Faith of Our Fathers

A Baptist Catechism for the Emerging New Breed

by Charles Middleton

Unless otherwise indicated, all Scripture quotations are taken from the *King James Version* of the Bible.

The Scripture quotation marked NASB is taken from *New American Standard Bible*. Copyright © 1960, 1962, 1963, 1968, 1971, 1972, 1973, 1975, 1977, 1995 by The Lockman Foundation, La Habra, California.

Scripture quotations marked (NLT) are taken from the *Holy Bible, New Living Translation*, copyright © 1996. Used by permission of Tyndale House Publishers, Inc., Wheaton, Illinois 60189. All rights reserved.

The Scripture quotation marked NRSV is taken from *The New Revised Standard Version of the Bible*. Copyright © 1946. Old Testament Section copyright © 1952 by The Division of Christian Education of the Churches of Christ in the United States of America. Concordances copyrighted by Thomas Nelson.

The Scripture quotation marked NIV is taken from *The Holy Bible: New International Version*. Copyright © 1973, 1978, 1984 by The International Bible Society. Used by permission of Zondervan Bible Publishers.

The Scripture quotations marked TLB are taken from *The Living Bible*. Copyright © 1971, 1988 by Tyndale House Publishers, Inc., Wheaton, Illinois.

Faith of Our Fathers — A Baptist Catechism for the Emerging New Breed
ISBN 978-1-946180-16-2
Copyright © 2012 by
Middleton and Middleton Ministries
8231 Second Avenue Detroit, Michigan 48202

Revised edition: 2019

Cover and Text Design:
Bobby and Lisa Simpson
www.simpsonproductions.net

Printed in the United States of America. All rights reserved under International Copyright Law. Contents and/or cover may not be reproduced in whole or in part in any form without the express written consent of the Author.

Contents

History of the National Baptist Convention 5
What We Believe 11
Study Course Mechanics 19

Beginnings — Section One

Lesson One The Christian Guidebook 27

Lesson Two The One True God 37

Lesson Three The Man That God Made 43

Lesson Four The Origin, Nature, and Effects of Sin 51

The Lord of the New Covenant — Section Two

Lesson Five Jesus Christ: Who Is He? 61

Lesson Six Jesus Christ: What Has He Done? 67

Lesson Seven What's in It for Me? 75

Lesson Eight Good News for Modern Man 85

Foundation Stones — Section Three

Lesson Nine Repentance From Dead Works 97

Lesson Ten Faith Toward God 103

Lesson Eleven The Doctrine of Baptisms: Into the Body of Christ 111

Lesson Twelve The Doctrine of Baptisms: Into Water 117

Lesson Thirteen THE DOCTRINE OF BAPTISMS: INTO THE HOLY SPIRIT.........125

Lesson Fourteen THE LAYING ON OF HANDS 135

Lesson Fifteen RESURRECTION OF THE DEAD 143

Lesson Sixteen: ETERNAL JUDGMENT 155

The Redeemed Community — Section Four

Lesson Seventeen THE NEW COVENANT CHURCH 169

Lesson Eighteen THE MEETING AND MISSION OF THE CHURCH..................187

Lesson Nineteen THE SACRAMENTS OF THE CHURCH 205

Lesson Twenty THE SACRAMENT OF CONFIRMATION 213

Lesson Twenty-One THE SACRAMENT OF HOLY COMMUNION....................219

Lesson Twenty-Two THE SACRAMENT OF FOOT WASHING 231

Lesson Twenty-Three THE SACRAMENT OF MATRIMONY............................241

Lesson Twenty-Four THE SACRAMENT OF THE DEDICATION OF CHILDREN 257

Lesson Twenty-Five THE SACRAMENT OF ANOINTING WITH OIL 267

Lesson Twenty-Six CHRISTIAN STEWARDSHIP...277

ENDNOTES 289

HISTORY OF THE NATIONAL BAPTIST CONVENTION

The National Baptist Convention, USA, Inc. traces a history of significant growth and achievements, attended sometimes by periods of turbulence, to Saturday, November 22, 1880 when 151 persons from 11 states met in Montgomery, Alabama and organized the Baptist Foreign Mission Convention. A yearning to see the Gospel of Jesus Christ preached on the Mother Soil of Africa drove this organizing. The Rev. W. H. McAlpine of Alabama was elected as its first President.

Six years later in 1886, 600 delegates from 17 states gathered at the First Baptist Church in St. Louis, Missouri and formed the National Baptist Convention of America. Seven years later in 1893, the National Baptist Education Convention was formed.

None of the three Conventions thrived separately. So in 1895, the three bodies effected a merger in a meeting held at the Friendship Baptist Church in Atlanta, Georgia. The Reverend E. C. Morris from Little Rock, Arkansas was chosen as the president of this merged body. Prior to 1895, nine men served as president of the Convention. Since 1895, eight men have led this venerable Convention.

Dr. Morris led for 28 years until 1922. During those years, a Publishing Board was established. At the direction of the Convention, the task was assigned to a Publishing Committee under the oversight of the Convention's Home Mission Board, led by the Reverend R. H. Boyd. Contentions developed around the issue of the independence of the Publishing Board. The Convention maintained that the Board was accountable to the Convention. The Board took an opposite posture. The disagreement led to a division in 1915, the Publishing Board and its supporters organized the National Baptist Convention of America un-incorporated. The Convention incorporated as the National Baptist Convention, USA, Inc. The incorporated body then established its own Publishing Board. It purchased land at 4th and Charlotte in downtown Nashville on the site once occupied by The Old Commercial Hotel. The Board erected a magnificent structure designed by the Negro architectural firm of McKissack & McKissack. The Building, when finished and furnished, was dedicated in 1926. Under Dr. Morris' leadership, the Baptist Young People's Union, the Women's Convention Auxiliary, the National Baptist Benefit Association and the Sunday School Congress were organized.

President, 1922-1940 Dr. L. K. Williams succeeded Dr. Morris as president in 1922. He organized the Laymen's Department, dedicated the Publishing Board Building and named it the Morris Memorial Building in honor of E. C. Morris. In 1925, the Convention, in collaboration with the Southern Baptist Convention, organized the American Baptist Theological Seminary. Dr. Williams died in a plane crash in 1940 and was succeeded by the Reverend D. V. Jemison. Under Dr. Jemison's guidance, the mortgage on the Morris Memorial Building was liquidated and a Bath House Hotel was purchased in Hot Springs, Arkansas.

Dr. D.V. Jemison retired from office in 1953 and the Reverend J.H. Jackson from Chicago, Illinois was elected president. Dr. Jackson served longer than any of his predecessors' holding office for 29 years. Differing concepts about engagement in the Civil Rights struggle and differing postures on term limitations for the president led to a division in the Convention and resulted in the formation of the Progressive National Baptist Convention. Dr. Jackson's unusual skill as a homiletician allowed him to become a world religious statesman who not spoke for the Convention, but for some in the community as well. His theme "We Must Move from Protest to Production," was characteristic of his thinking. Under Dr. Jackson, the Convention's accomplishments were many, including the purchase of a Freedom Farm in Tennessee to provide haven for Black farmers divested of their land in the civil rights revolution.

In 1982, Dr. T. J. Jemison challenged Dr. Jackson for the presidency of the Convention and was elected the 13th president of the Convention in Miami, Florida. Dr. Jemison led the Convention in the erection of the Baptist World Center as Convention Headquarters. It is an impressive structure located on twelve acres of land adjacent to American Baptist College.

During Dr. Jemison's term, the Convention voted to limit all officers of the Parent Body and its auxiliaries to a maximum of two consecutive five-year terms. So in the election of 1994, the Reverend Henry J. Lyons of St. Petersburg, Florida became the Convention's 14th president. Dr. Lyons reduced the mortgage on the Baptist World Center from 6 million dollars to 2.9 million dollars.

Unfortunately, because of alleged and self-confessed fiscal and moral improprieties, Dr. Lyons was forced to resign from office, leaving the Convention's spirit and reputation bruised. Dr. Lyons was succeeded by the Vice President-at-Large, The Reverend S. C. Cureton from South Carolina. Dr. Cureton finished Dr. Lyons term, but did not seek election to a five year period of his own. He provided a steady hand for the election of 1999 where the Reverend Dr. William J. Shaw of Philadelphia,

Pennsylvania was elected the 16th president of the National Baptist Convention, USA, Inc. Dr. Shaw was re-elected in 2004 with 68 percent of the votes cast.

During the 10 years of President Shaw's administration, the Convention was led to embrace VISA--an acronym for a set of Christ-centered leadership principles for establishing Vision, Integrity, Structure and Accountability. Under VISA, and the theme, "Jesus Christ Only, Always," the Convention's image and integrity were restored. Under Shaw's leadership, the mortgage on the Baptist World Center was liquidated in three years, a new Convention governance document was adopted, a Convention retirement program for pastors and church employees was established, a technology ministry & new website was launched, a focus on international ecumenical relations was begun, and a mechanism for organizing member response to natural disasters was established. Dr. Shaw also established an agenda of working together with other Baptist conventions in the United States. Toward this end, significant achievements during his administration included the historic convening of the four major black Baptist conventions (NBC, USA, Inc., National Baptist Convention of America, Progressive National Baptist Convention, and the National Missionary Baptist Convention of America), in 2004 and 2008; and joining with the New Baptist Covenant with a membership that includes Baptists from all ethnic and racial origins in the United States.

In September of 2009, the body elected a new Baptist Chieftain as its seventeenth president, the Reverend Dr. Julius Richard Scruggs. His platform was founded on the theme, "Solidarity With the Savior." The mandate for this servant was overwhelming for more than 75% of the vote was cast in favor of Dr. Scruggs. He had served the Convention as Vice-President at-large during the Shaw Administration. His campaign theme of "Solidarity with the Savior" will reflect the Christ-centered ecclesiology that will guide his administration.

In September 2014, Dr. Jerry Young was elected the eighteenth president. Dr. Young served as the Vice-President-At-Large under both the Shaw and Scruggs administrations. Dr. Young's platform theme is, "Envisioning the Future Exceptionally."

From humble beginnings in 1880 with only 151 delegates, and in spite of several major splits, the National Baptist Convention, USA, Inc. remains the largest black Baptist convention, counting millions of members from churches, district associations and state conventions across the Continental United States and around the world.

What We Believe

Articles of Faith

I. The Scriptures.

We believe that the Holy Bible was written by men divinely inspired, and is a perfect treasure of heavenly instruction; that it has God for its author, salvation for its end, and truth without any mixture of error for its matter; that it reveals the principles by which God will judge us, and therefore is, and shall remain to the end of the world, the true center of Christian union, and the supreme standard by which all human conduct, creeds, and opinions shall be tried.

II. The True God.

We believe the Scriptures teach that there is one, and only one, living and true God, an infinite, intelligent Spirit, whose name is Jehovah, the Maker and Supreme Ruler of heaven and earth; inexpressibly glorious in holiness, and worthy of all possible honor confidence and love; that in the unity of the Godhead there are three persons, the Father, the Son, and the Holy Ghost; equal in every divine perfection, and executing distinct but harmonious offices in the great work of redemption.

III. The Fall of Man.

We believe the Scriptures teach that Man was created in holiness, under the law of his Maker; but by voluntary transgressions fell from that holy and happy state; in consequence of which all mankind are now sinners, not by constraint but choice; being by nature utterly void of that holiness required by the law of God, positively inclined to evil; and therefore under just condemnation to eternal ruin, without defense or excuse.

IV. The Way of Salvation.

We believe that the Scriptures teach that the salvation of sinners is wholly of grace; through the mediatorial offices of the Son of God; who by the appointment of the Father, freely took upon him our nature, yet without sin; honored the divine law by his personal obedience, and by his death made a full atonement for our sins; that having risen from the dead, he is now enthroned in heaven; and uniting in his wonderful person the tenderest sympathies with divine perfections, he is in every way qualified to be a suitable, a compassionate, and an all-sufficient Savior.

V. Justification.

We believe the Scriptures teach that the great Gospel blessing which Christ secures to such as believe in him is justification; that justification includes the pardon of sin, and the promise of eternal life on principles of righteousness; that it is bestowed, not in consideration of any works of righteousness which we have done, but solely through faith in the Redeemer's blood; by virtue of which faith his perfect righteousness is freely imputed to us of God; that it brings us into a state of most blessed peace and favor with God, and secures every other blessing needful for time and eternity.

VI. The Freeness of Salvation.

We believe that the Scriptures teach that the blessings of salvation are made free to all by the Gospel; that it is the immediate duty of all to accept them by cordial, penitent and obedient faith; and that nothing prevents the salvation of the greatest sinner on earth, but his own determined depravity and voluntary rejection of the Gospel; which rejection involves him in an aggravated condemnation.

VII. Regeneration.

We believe that the Scriptures teach that in order to be saved, sinners must be regenerated, or born again; that regeneration consists in giving a holy disposition to the mind that it is effected in a manner above our comprehension by the power of the Holy Spirit in connection with divine truth, so as to secure our voluntary obedience to the Gospel; and that its proper evidence appears in the holy fruits of repentance and faith, and newness of life.

VIII. Repentance and Faith.

We believe the Scriptures teach that repentance and faith are sacred duties, and also inseparable graces, wrought in our souls by the regenerating Spirit of God; whereby being deeply convinced of our guilt, danger and helplessness and of the way of salvation by Christ, we turn to God with unfeigned contrition, confession, and supplication for mercy; at the same time heartily receiving the Lord Jesus Christ as our prophet, priest and king, and relying on him alone as the only and all-sufficient Savior.

IX. God's Purpose of Grace.

We believe the Scriptures teach that election is the eternal purpose of God, according to which he graciously regenerates, sanctifies and saves sinners; that being perfectly consistent with the free agency of man, it comprehends all the means in connection with the end; that it is a most glorious display of God's sovereign goodness, being infinitely free, wise, holy and unchangeable; that it utterly excludes boasting and promotes humility, love, prayer, praise, trust in God, and active imitation of his free mercy; that it encourages the use of means in the highest degree; that it may be ascertained by its effects in all who truly believe the Gospel; that it is the foundation of Christian assurance; and that to ascertain it with regard to ourselves demands and deserves the utmost diligence.

X. Sanctification.

We believe the Scriptures teach that Sanctification is the process by which, according to the will of God, we are made partakers of his holiness; that it is a progressive work; that it is begun in regeneration; and that it is carried on in the hearts of believers by the presence and power of the Holy Spirit, the Sealer and Comforter, in the continual use of the appointed means especially the word of God, self-examination, self-denial, watchfulness, and prayer.

XI. Perseverance of the Saints.

We believe the Scriptures teach that such only are real believers as endure to the end; that their persevering attachment to Christ is the grand mark which distinguishes them from superficial professors; that a special Providence watches over their welfare; and they are kept by the power of God through faith unto salvation.

XII. The Law and Gospel.

We believe the Scriptures teach that the Law of God is the eternal and unchangeable rule of his moral government; that it is holy, just and good; and that the inability which the Scriptures ascribe to fallen men to fulfill its precepts, arise entirely from their love of sin; to deliver them from which, and to restore them through a Mediator to unfeigned obedience to the holy Law, is one great end of the Gospel, and of the Means of Grace connected with the establishment of the visible church.

XIII. A Gospel Church.

We believe the Scriptures teach that a visible church of Christ is a congregation of baptized believers, associated by covenant in the faith and fellowship of the Gospel; observing the ordinances of Christ; governed by his laws; and exercising the gifts, rights, and privileges invested in them by His Word; that its only scriptural officers are Bishops or Pastors, and Deacons whose Qualifications, claims and duties are defined in the Epistles to Timothy and Titus.

XIV. Baptism and the Lord's Supper.

We believe the Scriptures teach that Christian baptism is the immersion in water of a believer, into the name of the Father, and Son, and Holy Ghost; to show forth in a solemn and beautiful emblem, our faith in the crucified, buried, and risen Savior, with its effect, in our death to sin and resurrection to a new life; that it is prerequisite to the privileges of a church relation; and to the Lord's Supper, in which the members of the church, by the sacred use of bread and wine, are to commemorate together the dying love of Christ; preceded always by solemn self-examination.

XV. The Christian Sabbath.

We believe the Scriptures teach that the first day of the week is the Lord's Day, or Christian Sabbath, and is to be kept sacred to religious purposes, by abstaining from all secular labor and sinful recreations, by the devout observance of all the means of grace, both private and public, and by preparation for that rest that remaineth for the people of God.

XVI. Civil Government.

We believe the Scriptures teach that civil government is of divine appointment, for the interest and good order of human society; and that magistrates are to be prayed for, conscientiously honored and obeyed; except only in things opposed to the will of our Lord Jesus Christ, who is the only Lord of the conscience, and the Prince of the Kings of the earth.

XVII. Righteous and Wicked.

We believe the Scriptures teach that there is a radical and essential difference between the righteous and the wicked; that such only as through faith are justified in the name of the Lord Jesus, and sanctified by the Spirit of our God, are truly righteous in his esteem; while all such as continue in impenitence and unbelief are in his sight wicked, and under the curse; and this distinction holds among men both in and after death.

XVIII. The World to Come.

We believe the Scriptures teach that the end of the world is approaching; that at the last day, Christ will descend from heaven, and raise the dead from the grave for final retribution; that a solemn separation will then take place; that the wicked will be adjudged to endless punishment, and the righteous to endless joy; and that this judgment will fix forever the final state of men in heaven or hell, on principles of righteousness.

Statement of Religious Freedom

October 2010

The National Baptist Convention, USA, Inc. believes that religious liberty is a gift from God. We support the freedom of the individual conscience to choose to worship God according to the dictates of one's heart. And while we celebrate our own liberty to embrace biblical truth without compromise, we also support the first amendment to the Constitution which guarantees freedom of religion for all Americans. In this light, as Americans, we join with other faith communities in supporting the right of Islamic and other religious bodies to worship according to the dictates and mandates of their faith expressions.

STUDY COURSE MECHANICS

1. ATTENDANCE

Because of the subject matter in this course, it is important that each student make a special effort to attend every session. It is necessary to keep absenteeism at a minimum. More than three absences will affect confirmation.

2. CLASSES

Each class period will include a praise and worship experience and a 45minute teaching session. After the teaching session, counseling groups should convene for further discussion of questions and answers. Thirty minutes is enough time for this gathering.

3. LESSON

Each student should read the lesson at least once

before class in order to get the best results from the

study. Also, look up all scriptural references.

4. HOMEWORK

At the end of each lesson, a set of study questions will be handed out. Students must write out all answers to the questions (as the textbook explains them). Homework will be due each week, and must be handed in at the beginning of the teaching session. When study questions have been graded and returned, check to see whether or not your homework was marked satisfactory. If it is *unsatisfactory,* it must be done again.

5. TEST

At the end of the course, a final test will be given.

In case of unsatisfactory work, you will be given

another chance to retake the test.

6. CONFIRMATION

This will be done by the laying on of the hands of

the local church leaders after the class is completed.

CONFIRMATION IS ONLY FOR THOSE WHO HAVE:

(1) Evidenced or demonstrated a real experience of Salvation, Water Baptism, and the Baptism in the Holy Spirit.

(2) Turned in all homework assignments.

(3) Successfully completed every quiz and the final test.

Beginnings

Section One

GOALS AND OBJECTIVES

1. Understand the true standard of faith and practice
2. Know the One True God
3. Know the natural and spiritual destiny of the man that God made
4. Know the sin problem, according to scripture

We have a mandate in this hour to do at least two things: 1) Liberate the Christian faith from it's cultural captivity, and 2) Craft a fullorbed Christian world view and pass it on to the next generation. This study is a major step in the direction of fulfilling this task.

Lesson One

2 Timothy 3:14-17 NLT

14 But you must remain faithful to the things you have been taught. You know they are true, for you know you can trust those who taught you.

15 You have been taught the holy Scriptures from childhood, and they have given you the wisdom to receive the salvation that comes by trusting in Christ Jesus.

16 All Scripture is inspired by God and is useful to teach us what is true and to make us realize what is wrong in our lives. It straightens us out and teaches us to do what is right.

17 It is God's way of preparing us in every way, fully equipped for every good thing God wants us to do.

THE CHRISTIAN GUIDEBOOK

We believe that the whole Bible was given to us by inspiration from God. We judge everything by what the Bible says. Actually, we live by the Bible because it is the Word of God.

1. WHAT IS THE "HOLY BIBLE"?

The "Holy Bible" is a collection of writings written by saintly men, who were "moved by the Spirit of God." The Bible consists of sixtysix books in all.

For the prophecy came not in old time by the will of man: but holy men of God spake as they were moved by the Holy Ghost.

2 Peter 1:21

2. HOW MANY PARTS IS THE BIBLE DIVIDED INTO?

There are two major divisions into which the Bible is divided. The Old Testament contains thirtynine books, and preserves the Word of God that was revealed to mankind through the prophets before the coming of our Savior, Jesus Christ. The New Testament consists of twentyseven books and preserves the Word of God that was revealed to mankind by Jesus Christ and the holy apostles.

WE BELIEVE THAT GOD WATCHED OVER THE PEOPLE WHO WROTE THE SCRIPTURES, SO THAT NO ONE MADE ANY MISTAKES.

3. **WHAT ARE SOME IMPORTANT THINGS THAT WE MUST DO AS CHRISTIANS?**

   A. We must accept God's Word for what it really is. God gives us His Word to protect us, to make us wise, to make us free, to guide us, and to give us health (Psalms 19:710, 107:20; 119:9,130).

Jesus said to the people who believed in him, "You are truly my disciples if you keep obeying my teachings.

And you will know the truth, and the truth will set you free."

John 8:31-32 NLT

   B. We must walk in the light of what the Word of God says.

But be ye doers of the word, and not hearers only, deceiving your own selves.

For if any be a hearer of the word, and not a doer, he is like unto a man beholding his natural face in a glass:

For he beholdeth himself, and goeth his way, and straightway forgetteth what manner of man he was.

But whoso looketh into the perfect law of liberty, and continueth therein, he being not a forgetful hearer, but a doer of the work, this man shall be blessed in his deed.

James 1:22-25

C. We must study the Scriptures to find out the following things:

(1) What our heavenly Father did for us when Jesus died on the cross. (Cp. Romans 3:2 ff; Galatians 3:13; 1 Peter 2:24; 1 John 3:8.)

(2) What it means to be a real Christian. (Cp. Acts 11:26; Ephesians 5:120; James 1:2627; 1 Peter 2:910.)

(3) What we have and what we can do as members of the family of God. (Cp. Mark 16:1520; Luke 10:19; Philippians 4:13; James 4:7.)

4. ARE THERE ANY BLACK PEOPLE IN THE BIBLE?

Actually, the Bible is a book for all humanity, but it is especially a book for black people.

A. African territories are mentioned in the Bible:

1. Egypt (Genesis 12:1014; Revelation 11:8)
2. Libya (Ezekiel 30:5; Daniel 11:43; Acts 2:10)
3. Ethiopia (Genesis 2:13; 2 Kings 19:9; Psalm 68:31)
4. Alexandria (Acts 6:9, 18:24, 27:6, 28:11)
5. Cyrene (Matthew 27:32; Acts 2:10, 11:20, 13:1)

B. People of African origin are mentioned in the Old and New Testaments:

1. Nimrod (Genesis 10:614)

2. Jethro (Exodus 18:1)

3. Zipporah (Numbers 12:1)

4. Hagar (Genesis 21:13)

5. Asenath, Manasseh, and Ephraim (Genesis 41:45, 46:20)

6. The Queen of Sheba (1 Kings 10:1013)

7. Cushi (Zephaniah 1:1)

8. Lucius of Cyrene (Acts 13:1)

9. Simeon of Niger (Acts 13:1)

10. Rufus (Mark 15:21; Romans 16:13)

11. Study also Amos 9:7a and Isaiah 19:2325.

5. ARE THERE ANY GOOD SUMMARY STATEMENTS OF OUR FAITH?

The heart or essence of our faith, as contained in the Holy Bible, is found in The African Creed that the apostles gave in Jerusalem – "THE AMAKNIYOU OF THE APOSTLES," and in the creed set forth in the council of NICEA in AD 325. These symbols of faith were composed primarily by African church leaders for the Church of Jesus Christ at large.

6. WHY WERE THE CREEDS COMPOSED?

Basically, these creeds were composed and given to every Christian so they would not stray from the truth.

7. WHAT IS THE TEXT OF THE CREEDS?

AMAKNIYOU

A. AMAKNIYOU OF THE APOSTLES

We believe in one God, Maker of all creation, Father of our Lord and our Savior Jesus Christ, because His nature is unsearchable.

As we have before declared, He is without beginning and without end, but He is ever living, and He has light which is never extinguished and He can never be approached.

He is not two or three, and no addition can be made to Him; but He is only one, living forever, because He is not hidden that He cannot be known, but we know Him perfectly through the law and the prophets, that He is Almighty and has authority over all the creations.

One God, Father of our Savior Jesus Christ, who was begotten before the creation of the world, the only begotten Son, coequal with Him, Creator of all the hosts, the principalities, and the dominions.

Who in the last days was pleased to become man, and took flesh from our lady Mary, the Holy Virgin, without the seed of man, and grew like men yet without sin or evil; neither was guile found in His mouth.

Then He suffered, died in the flesh, rose from the dead on the third day, ascended into Heaven to the Father who sent Him, sat down at the right hand of power, sent to us the Paraclete, the Holy Spirit, who proceeded from the Father, and provided salvation for all the world, and who is coeternal with the Father and the Son.

We say further that all the creatures of God are good and there is nothing to be rejected, and the spirit, the life of the body is pure and holy in all.

And we say that marriage is pure and childbirth is undefiled, because God created Adam and Eve to multiply. We understand further that there is in our body a soul which is immortal and does not perish with the body.

We repudiate all works of heretics and all schisms and transgressions of the law, because they are impure for us.

We also believe in the resurrection of the dead, the righteous and sinners; and in the day of Judgment, when everyone will be recompensed according to his deeds.

We also believe that Christ is not in the least degree inferior because of His Incarnation, but He is God, the Word who truly became man and reconciled mankind to God being the High Priest of the Father. Henceforth, let us not be circumcised like the Jews. We know that He who had to fulfill the law and the prophets has already come.

To Him, for whose coming all people looked forward, Jesus Christ, who is descended from Judah, from the root of Jesse, whose government is upon His shoulder: to Him be glory, thanksgiving, greatness, blessing, praise, song, both now and forever and world without end. Amen.

THE NICEAN CREED OF 325 A.D.

B. THE NICENE CREED OF A.D. 325

I believe in one God, the Father Almighty, Maker of Heaven and Earth, and of all things visible and invisible;

And in one Lord Jesus Christ, the Son of God, the Only begotten, begotten of the Father before all worlds, Light of Light, Very God of Very God, begotten, not made; of one essence with the Father, by Whom all things were made:

Who for us men and for our salvation came down from Heaven, and was incarnate of the Holy Spirit and the Virgin Mary, and was made man;

And was crucified also for us under Pontius Pilate, and suffered and was buried;

And the third day He rose again, according to the Scriptures;

And ascended into Heaven, and sits at the right hand of the Father;

And He shall come again with glory to judge the living and the dead, whose Kingdom shall have no end.

And I believe in the Holy Spirit, the Lord, and Giver of life, who proceeds from the Father, who with the Father and the Son together is worshipped and glorified, who spoke by the prophets;

And I believe in one Holy Catholic and Apostolic Church.

I acknowledge one baptism for the remission of sins.

I look for the resurrection of the dead,

And the life of the world to come. Amen.

8. WHAT DO WE LEARN IN THESE CREEDS?

In the articles of these symbols of faith, we especially learn about:

A. The One True God.

B. The life to come.

C. The Church and its mission.

Conclusion

All in all, the Christian Guidebook is the Holy Bible. It is the Word of God. It is perfect and complete. It has the power to restore the soul and to give wisdom. The Word of God is right and pure. It will enlighten the eyes, and make your heart happy and clean. More than anything, we should desire to study God's Word for all it is worth.

Lesson Two

Deuteronomy 6:4‑5 NASB

4 "Hear, O Israel! The LORD is our God, the LORD is one!

5 "You shall love the LORD your God with all your heart and with all your soul and with all your might."

The One True God

In the first book of the Bible, in the first chapter and the first verse of that book, the One True God is revealed:

In the beginning God created the heaven and the earth.

Genesis 1:1

No explanation is given of His existence. He simply shows up unannounced, and we accept His revelation by faith seeking understanding.

9. DOES THE BIBLE GIVE US A DEFINITION OF GOD?

The best definition of God that anyone can really understand is found in the writings of John, the beloved disciple of Jesus Christ. This is what he says:

A. "God is Spirit, and we must have his help to worship as we should" (John 4:24 TLB).

B. "God is LIGHT, and in him is no darkness at all" (1 John 1:5).

C. "If a person ISN'T loving and kind, it shows that he doesn't know God—for GOD IS LOVE" (1 John 4:8 TLB).

10. ARE THERE MORE GODS THAN ONE?

The correct answer to this question is NO! There is only One True God (Isaiah 45:56), and He is fully explained by Jesus Christ (John 1:18).

11. **IN WHAT WAYS HAS GOD REVEALED HIMSELF TO US?**

    A. God has revealed Himself as "our Father" (John 1:12 ff., 20:17).

    B. God has revealed Himself as "the Word" and as "the Son of God" (John 1:12,14; Colossians 2:9; Hebrews 1:13).

    C. God has revealed Himself as "The Holy Spirit" (Matthew 28:19; 2 Corinthians 3:17, 13:14; Genesis 1:2).

    This is a great mystery! God is essentially one, but He reveals Himself in many ways.

12. **WHAT ARE SOME OF THE MAIN CHARACTERISTICS OF GOD?**

    A. God is *Almighty!* (Cp. Genesis 17:1; Matthew 19:26)

    B. God is *everywhere!* (Cp. Psalm 139:712)

    C. God *knows everything!* (Cp. 1 John 3:20; Psalm 139:4)

    D. God is *absolutely pure!* (Cp. Leviticus 19:2)

    E. God is *a good God!* (Cp. Psalm 145:9)

    F. God is *merciful!* (Cp. Jeremiah 3:12; Luke 6:36)

    G. God is always *fair* and *just!* (Cp. Deuteronomy 32:4)

    H. God always *keeps His promises!* (Cp. 2 Timothy 2:13)

13. **WHAT DO THE CREEDS TELL US ABOUT THE ONE TRUE GOD?**

    These early symbols of faith identify the One True God in the following ways:

A. He is "God the Father Almighty." This means that God is the ground and source of our lives. We are His offspring (John 1:12).

B. He is "The Maker of Heaven and Earth." This means that atheistic evolution is wrong. The Father Almighty is the Maker of Heaven and Earth.

14. DOES GOD HAVE A NAME?

In the Old Testament, God is called by many names: "The Almighty," "The Most High," and "The Lord" are but a few (Genesis 14:18, 17:1; Exodus 3:1415). In the New Testament, God is revealed in "the Lord Jesus Christ." We could say that God's name is Jesus!

For it pleased the Father that in him should all fulness dwell.

Colossians 1:19

For in him dwelleth all the fulness of the Godhead bodily. And ye are complete in him, which is the head of all principality and power.

Colossians 2:910

Conclusion

The One true God, who is worshipped in Spirit and in truth, is revealed in the beautiful world of planets, stars, trees, waters, and flowers. Supremely, He is revealed in Jesus Christ – His Son and our Lord.

Because we are the children of God, we trust Him with all of our hearts. He is our Father, Almighty. He is the Maker of Heaven and Earth. There is none like Him; thus, we ascribe to

Him greatness. He is the Rock! His work is perfect, and all of His ways are just. He's a God of faithfulness, and He's without injustice. Good and upright is what He is.

Lesson Three

GENESIS 1:26-27

26 And God said, Let us make man in our image, after our likeness: and let them have dominion over the fish of the sea, and over the fowl of the air, and over the cattle, and over all the earth, and over every creeping thing that creepeth upon the earth.

27 So God created man in his own image, in the image of God created he him; male and female created he them.

THE MAN THAT GOD MADE

The original man was made by God and was in many ways just like God. The Bible says it like this:

So God created man in his own image, in the image of God created he him; male and female created he them.

Genesis 1:27

15. WHAT IS THE IMAGE OF GOD?

To be in God's image and likeness means to be "good and upright and intelligent." God is like this and so is the person who has His image and likeness. The image and likeness of God also mean "acting and thinking like God." The Scriptures teach that Jesus Christ was the exact image of God. He acted just like His heavenly Father (Ephesians 4:1213,24; Colossians 3:10; Hebrews 1:3, 6:1).

16. DOES MANKIND STILL HAVE THE IMAGE OF GOD?

According to the Bible, even though sin has corrupted and perverted everything, all is not lost. Even in the lowest heathen, something of the image of God can be seen. This is why all men and women have the right to life, freedom, and the pursuit of happiness. It's because every person is made in the likeness and image of God. On the inside (in his heart or spirit) mankind has the image and likeness of God, but what about his physical body?

17. WHAT COLOR WAS ADAM AND EVE?

Actually, the Bible gives us some clues as to the color of the original people. In Genesis 2:7 we learn that Adam was formed from the soil. There is no white dirt or soil anywhere on earth. The richest soil is black or reddishbrown. In the Hebrew language, the name "Adam" means reddishbrown. So, the color of Adam and Eve was probably reddishbrown.

18. WHY WOULD ARTISTS PAINT PICTURES OF ADAM AND EVE AND COLOR THEM WHITE?

Unfortunately, racism has been a problem in Europe and America for a long time. This is no doubt the reason why there are so many pictures of a white Adam and Eve.

Note: Secular anthropologists and scientists, who recently published their findings in *Newsweek* and *National Geographic,* agreed that Adam and Eve were African or dark. See *Newsweek* magazine, January 11, 1988.

19. WHAT ABOUT THE GARDEN OF EDEN? DO WE KNOW WHERE IT IS LOCATED?

Africa is the real cradle of civilization. Life on earth began in "Old [classical] Africa." Thanks to the research of the late Dr. Louis Leaky, we know that the birthplace of mankind was in East Africa's Great Lakes region, around the OMO valley. This is almost right on the equator.

The Bible also identified the Garden of Eden with four rivers: The Pishon, Gihon, Tigris, and the Euphrates (Genesis 2:1014). See the map!

20. HOW IS AFRICA REFERRED TO IN THE BIBLE?

In Psalms 78:51 and 105:23, Africa is called "The Land of Ham." The patriarch Jacob wandered all of his life in "The Land of Ham," which was also called "Canaan" or "The Promised Land" (Psalm 49:11).

Note: Were you aware of the fact that there was an Ethiopian man named Havilah? His father was Cush (the father of the Ethiopians). Read Genesis 10:7. Does this insight help you locate Havilah on the map?

21. WHAT ABOUT THE AFRICAN CIVILIZATION? WHAT ABOUT THE ETHIOPIAN EMPIRE?

The Ethiopian Empire was one of the largest empires to ever rule the world. It was rich in many ways. Ancient records show that the alphabet, geometry, architecture, engineering, and the use of herbs in medicine can be traced to Africa. Also, much of the metals and minerals valued throughout the world are mined in Africa. It is a fact that European civilization and culture borrowed a lot from our African forefathers.

22. WHAT ARE SOME WAYS IN WHICH BOYS AND GIRLS ARE ALIKE?

The Bible is clear on this point. There are at least ten ways in which boys and girls are alike. Observe!

Both were:

A. Created by God.

B. Created in God's image.

C. Created for God's glory.

D. Created to worship God.

E. Created spirit, soul, and body.

F. Blessed by God.

G. Given authority and dominion over the earth.

H. Responsible for their own behavior.

I. Able to make their own decisions.

J. Made to need each other.

23. IN WHAT WAYS ARE BOYS AND GIRLS UNIQUE?

According to the Scriptures, boys are especially created to function as "the head." In other words, boys are to provide and protect. Girls, on the other hand, are especially created to function as "suitable helpers." Boys and girls are also unique in that boys are primarily givers, and girls are primarily receivers.

24. DOES THIS MEAN THAT BOYS ARE BETTER THAN GIRLS?

No! In God's eyes everybody is equal. The only difference is that we all have special ways that we are to function in life.

As many of you as were baptized into Christ have clothed yourselves with Christ.

There is no longer Jew or Greek, there is no longer slave or free, there is no longer male and female; for all of you are one in Christ Jesus.

Galatians 3:2728 NRSV

25. DOES THE BIBLE TEACH THAT MEN AND WOMEN ARE PARTNERS IN THE BUSINESS OF THE FATHER?

A. The unity and relatedness of Adam and Eve are seen in the fact that Eve was taken out of Adam's side.

B. The word "helper" (Genesis 2:18) is used fifteen times in the Old Testament to refer to God. Obviously, it cannot imply inferiority or subordination.

C. The principle of "equality in Christ" (Galatians 3:26-29) deserves more emphasis.

D. The Scriptures clearly say that men and women are to share rulership and dominion (Genesis 1:26).

26. CAN YOU EXPLAIN THE THREEFOLD MAKEUP OF MAN? STUDY THE DIAGRAM BELOW!

Based upon First Thessalonians 5:23, the nonmaterial part of man consists of a spirit and a soul. The material part of man consists of a physical body. The body is the worldconscious part of our being. The five senses (sight, touch, hearing, smell, and taste) give us an awareness of our natural surroundings. Our bodily appetites are a part of our physical and psychological makeup.

The human soul provides for selfconsciousness. The soul has three faculties: intellect, emotions, and willpower. Together, these make up the real person. The soul connects spirit and body and governs the whole personality.

We also have a spirit. God is Spirit (John 4:24). Our human spirit relates to the world of the unseen – the world of spirit (whether good or evil). We know the One True God in our spirit.

A person who is "spiritually dead" is separated from God in the spirit, and the realm of their understanding is darkened (Ephesians 2:110, 4:18).

Conclusion

This lesson is a powerful reminder that "we are fearfully and wonderfully made" (Psalm 139:14). God has actually brought us on the scene to reflect His character, wear His name, and exercise His authority in the earth. While there are many evil things in our world and culture that oppose our Godgiven identity and peace, in spite of this, we do have the image and likeness of God inside of us, and that makes us very special.

Lesson Four

Romans 3:9–18 NIV

9 What shall we conclude then? Are we any better? Not at all! We have already made the charge that Jews and Gentiles alike are all under sin.

10 As it is written: "There is no one righteous, not even one;

11 there is no one who understands, no one who seeks God.

12 All have turned away, they have together become worthless; there is no one who does good, not even one."

13 "Their throats are open graves; their tongues practice deceit. The poison of vipers is on their lips."

14 "Their mouths are full of cursing and bitterness."

15 "Their feet are swift to shed blood;

16 ruin and misery mark their ways,

17 and the way of peace they do not know."

18 "There is no fear of God before their eyes."

The Origin, Nature, and Effects of Sin

It is a fact that there's something seriously wrong with this world. Everything seems to be in a mess. It's everywhere. People don't seem to measure up. They are always missing the mark and breaking the rules. You can't trust anybody. But then again, it's not always other people. Sometimes, in your own heart you want to do dumb stuff. Sometimes you want to hurt people or be a racist. Sometimes you take advantage of people you love, and the list goes on. Yes, there is something seriously wrong with our world and everybody knows it.

27. DOES THE BIBLE EXPLAIN THIS PROBLEM

The story of the fall of Lucifer, one of God's highest ranking angels, explains the problem. Iniquity was found in Lucifer, and he desired to replace God as the king of the universe. He wanted to be worshipped (Isaiah 14:1215; Ezekiel 28:1317). Through slander, he influenced other angels to join him in his rebellion. God responded by casting Lucifer and his fellow rebels out of Heaven.

Lucifer then proceeds to set up his own kingdom of darkness. He did this for the sole purpose of frustrating the work of God in the earth (John 10:10; Ephesians 6:12; Hebrews 2:14; 1 Peter 5:8).

Another explanation of the problem is found in the story of Adam, Eve, and a shrewd serpent (who was really the devil). Adam and Eve were married to each other and lived in a beautiful gardenpark in East Africa called "Eden." Read the story in Genesis 2:3-3:24.

28. WHAT ARE THE MAIN POINTS OF THE STORY OF ADAM AND EVE AND THE SERPENT?

A. The first thing we learn in this story is that disobedience is serious business. God gave Adam and Eve some major responsibilities. They were to be productive, manage the garden estate, and obtain knowledge only from God. Both Adam and Eve disobeyed.

B. The next important point in the story is that the disobedience of Adam and his wife was brought on by the evil schemes of the devil (Genesis 3:1 ff.; Ephesians 6:11; 2 Timothy 2:14).

Note: Satan attacked God's Word. He questioned it. He denied it and caused doubt and confusion. He deceived Eve (Isaiah 14:1314).

29. WHAT ABOUT THE CONSQUENCES OF SIN? WHAT DOES THE BIBLE SAY?

A. The Bible teaches that when Adam and Eve disobeyed God, their nature changed from being "okay" to being corrupt (Ephesians 4:2224). Being corrupt, they became subject to death (1 Corinthians 15:5354).

B. The Bible also teaches that, as a result of disobedience, Satan "took over" (Genesis 1:26; Psalm 8:48; Luke 4:56; Ephesians 2:23).

C. Finally, because of disobedience, everything became subject to vanity and judgment (Genesis 3:1419; Romans 8:1823 with Romans 3:19).

30. WHAT HAS ALL OF THIS GOT TO DO WITH US TODAY?

The truth of the matter is that it has everything to do with us. The guilt and corruption that we see in Adam and Eve are in us. We are connected to them. They are our parents. We are their children. We are all in Adam's family, and we are bothered by all kinds of wrong things:

A. Pride

B. Envy

C. Hatred

D. Racism

E. Fear

F. Lust

G. Deceit

H. Evil desires

Like it or not, this is the way it is. The only way to deal with this problem is to get out of this crazy, mixedup Adam's family. It's tough, but it can happen. That's what Jesus is all about!

31. WHAT ELSE SHOULD WE EMPHASIZE?

First of all, we must emphasize the point that sin creates unjust social structures and destroys people. These structures may be political, economic, or cultural. They may even grow out of wrong attitudes based on race, class, nationality, or sexual gender. Sometimes these structures are embodied in churches and provide religious support for evil.

Secondly, we must emphasize the point that sin puts a person in bondage that's so deep that liberation seems impossible. For instance, if a person is born in poverty, slavery, or is weak, ignorant, and involved in homosexuality, then it would seem that nothing could be done about their situation. Sometimes the powerful persons and systems that control things suggest that it is the will of God that things can't change, and that you should stay in your place. This is good news for them, but bad news for the oppressed.

We shall see later on that the good news that Jesus brings is all about liberation from these impossible situations. His main message is that things do not have to stay the way they are. God is working to make things right. In other words, because of what God has done and because of what He is doing now, people whose lives are in a mess can have hope for a better day.

Conclusion

All in all, this lesson has been designed to show "the sinfulness of sin." Sin is nothing nice. It is a terrible employer that pays wages. The Bible calls those wages "death." Its origins go all the way back to Satan – the evil enemy of God Himself.

Sin creates social and political conditions that make life miserable. Only God, through His Son Jesus Christ, can bring real deliverance.

The Lord of the New Covenant

Section Two

GOALS AND OBJECTIVES

1. Know the unique Son of God.

2. Be able to explain His redemptive work.

3. Be able to rightly communicate the primary benefits of the atonement.

4. Begin to better appreciate the lordship of Jesus Christ.

If you are going to be effective as an able minister of the New Covenant, you must master this section. Accept its witness. Take hold of its benefits and always remember:

> "What think ye of Jesus?
> Neutral you cannot be.
> One day your soul will be asking,
> 'What will He do with me?'"

Lesson Five

Philippians 2:511 NLT

5 "Your attitude should be the same that Christ Jesus in heaven and on earth and under the earth,

6 Though he was God, he did not demand and cling to his rights as God.

7 He made himself nothing; he took the humble position of a slave and appeared in human form.

8 And in human form he obediently humbled himself even further by dying a criminal's death on a cross.

9 Because of this, God raised him up to the heights of heaven and gave him a name that is above every other name,

10 so that at the name of Jesus every knee will bow, in heaven and on earth and under the earth,

11 and every tongue will confess that Jesus Christ is Lord, to the glory of God the Father."

Jesus Christ: Who Is He?

The earliest Christians knew that Jesus was not like any other person. To them, He was "the only oneofakind" Son of God, and they never compromised this truth.

Jesus is also important to us today. What we believe about Him determines our relationships in life; plus, it determines our eternal destiny. This is why we approach this part of the Foundations Study Course with a special kind of attitude.

32. WHAT DOES THE NAME "JESUS" MEAN?

The name "Jesus" means, "God is SAVIOR." The angel explained to Mary why her baby was to have that name: "He will save his people from their sins." The Apostle Peter moreover says, "There is none other name under heaven given among men, whereby we must be saved."

Cp. Matthew 1:1823; Acts 4:12.

33. WHAT ABOUT THE WORD "CHRIST"? IS THIS JESUS' LAST NAME?

Actually the word "Christ" means "Anointed One" or "Messiah." Jesus was called "Christ" because "God anointed [Him] with the Holy Ghost and with power," and He was able to do good and heal all who were oppressed by the devil.

Cp. Acts 10:38.

34. WHAT DOES IT MEAN TO SAY THAT JESUS IS THE "SON OF GOD"?

This title signifies the unique and eternal relationship that Jesus Christ has with the Father. In a real sense, because Jesus is the Son of God, they have the same nature. They are one.

> Cp. John 1:1,14,18, 3:16,18; 1 John 2:23.

35. WHAT ABOUT THE TITLE "LORD"? IS JESUS THE LORD?

In the Old Testament Scriptures, "LORD" is the name by which the God of Israel is known.

In the New Testament, it is used in reference to the Father, and in reference to Jesus.

When early African believers called Jesus "Lord," they confessed that the power, honor and glory due to God the Father was also due to Jesus. Why? Because they saw that Jesus was "one with the Father," i.e., God was in Him.

> *34 "For David did not ascend into the heavens, but he says himself: 'The LORD said to my Lord, Sit at My right hand, 35 Till I make Your enemies Your footstool. 36 Therefore let all the house of Israel know assuredly that God has made this Jesus, whom you crucified, both Lord and Christ."*
>
> Acts 2:3436 NKJV

> *9 "Therefore God also has highly exalted Him and given Him the name which is above every name, 10 that at the name of Jesus every knee should bow, of those in heaven, and of those on earth, and of those under the earth, 11 and*

that every tongue should confess that Jesus Christ is Lord, to the glory of God the Father."

Philippians 2:9-11 NKJV

36. DID JESUS REALLY EXIST BEFORE HE WAS BORN?

This is a great mystery, but it is true. Jesus really did exist before He was born in Bethlehem!

- A. Jesus Himself claimed to be preexistent. "I AM" is a reference to the sacred name of God. Cp. John 8:58; Exodus 3:14-15.

- B. Jesus is said to have been involved in the work of creation. This can only mean that He existed before His birth.

- C. Jesus is called "The Word" in John 1:1. This means that He is the eternal utterance or expression of God. (See also John 1:18.)

37. WHY DO WE BELIEVE THAT JESUS IS GOD?

- A. The New Covenant name of the one true God is "LORD Jesus Christ." Cp. 2 Corinthians 5:19a.

16 "For by Him all things were created that are in heaven and that are on earth, visible and invisible, whether thrones or dominions or principalities or powers. All things were created through Him and for Him. 17 And He is before all things, and in Him all things consist."

Colossians 1:16-17 NKJV

- B. Jesus claimed to be equal with God. Cp. John 5:18.

- C. Jesus is said to do things that only God could do. Cp. Hebrews 1:3.

D. Divine glory and honor belong to Him. Cp. John 5:23.

38. WHY DO WE BELIEVE THAT THE LORD JESUS CHRIST WAS A REAL MAN?

Jesus was doubtlessly a real man for at least three reasons: He is referred to as "the man Christ Jesus" (1 Timothy 2:5). He had "human" feelings and experiences (sleeping, THE LORD OF THE NEW COVENANT crying, suffering, etc.) (John 11:33; Matthew 26:38). He had a human spirit, soul and body (Luke 24:39).

39. WHAT COLOR WAS JESUS?

We know that Jesus had "black blood in His veins." His family tree is made up of both Hamitic and Semitic people (descendants of Ham and Shem). By American legal standards, anyone with even a small amount of African ancestry is considered black. Flavius Josephus (Jewish historian) said, "Jesus was a man of plain looks, extremely learned and full of vigor, with dark skin."[1]

Conclusion

The bottom line is that Jesus was a Hamitic Jew. His earthly parents were of typical AfroAsiatic stock and had no problem hiding themselves and their "darkskinned" baby in Africa. Jesus had both a human nature and a divine nature that never was mixed or confounded so as to make a third nature. This qualified Him to be the true liberator of the entire human race.

---

[1]

Lesson Six

1 Corinthians 15:34 NLT

3 "I passed on to you what was most important and what had also been passed on to me — that Christ died for our sins, just as the Scriptures said.

4 He was buried, and he was raised from the dead on the third day, as the Scriptures said."

JESUS CHRIST: WHAT HAS HE DONE?

Many people believe that if they are going to experience the really good life they are going to have to make it happen themselves. The truth of the matter is that our experience of the "abundant life" (John 10:10) is really dependent upon Jesus Christ and what He has done.

40. DID JESUS HAVE A GODGIVEN JOB TO DO?

There was a clear sense of purpose in the heart of Jesus as He moved around among the people. He knew that God wanted Him to fulfill a particular assignment.

34 "Jesus said to them, 'My food is to do the will of Him who sent Me, and to finish His work.'"

John 4:34 NKJV

The Apostles explain the work of Jesus in their writing.

4 "I have glorified You on the earth. I have finished the work which You have given Me to do."

John 17:4 NKJV

7 "Then I said, 'Behold, I have come — In the volume of the book it is written of Me — To do Your will, O God."

Hebrews 10:7 NKJV

Here we learn that Jesus paid the penalty for our sins by His death on the cross and the shedding of His blood.

42. WHAT DO WE BELIEVE ABOUT THE DEATH OF JESUS CHRIST?

45 "For even I, the Son of Man, came here not to be served but to serve others, and to give my life as a ransom for many."

Mark 10:45 NLT

A. We believe that the death of Jesus Christ was endured, "in the place of others" (1 Corinthians 15:3).

B. We believe that the death of Jesus Christ satisfied the wrath of God the Father (Romans 3:25 NLT). God is NOT angry with us now.

C. We believe that the death of Jesus provided the way to totally remove or alleviate our sins. (Through Old Testament animal sacrifices, man's sins were "covered.") Through Jesus' death, burial and resurrection, provision was made for our sins to be removed (Exodus 29:3337; Leviticus 16:617; Matthew 26:28; Revelation 1:5).

D. We believe that the wounds and the death of Jesus provided healing for our physical bodies.

E. We believe that through His death, Jesus freed us from the curse of the Law.

4 "Surely He has borne our griefs and carried our sorrows; yet we esteemed Him stricken, smitten by God, and afflicted. 5 But He was wounded for our transgressions, He was bruised for our iniquities; the chastisement for our peace was upon Him, and by His stripes we are healed."

Isaiah 53:45 NKJV

Note! Read also, in this connection, the biblical revelation of the curse of the Law in Deuteronomy 28:1568.

> F. We believe that, in His death on the cross, Jesus demonstrates the love of God for humanity. He also shows us how we must demonstrate the same love for each other.

13 "Christ has redeemed us from the curse of the law, having become a curse for us (for it is written, 'Cursed is everyone who hangs on a tree')."

Galatians 3:13 NKJV

43. WHO DID JESUS DIE FOR?

The Bible teaches us that Jesus, by His death on the cross, made salvation possible for those who were especially given to Him by the Father (John 17:9). The Bible also teaches that Jesus made salvation possible for the whole world (John 3:16).

". . . Jesus Christ, in His death, became the perfect, pure, sinless sacrifice. He offered Himself to God as the atonement to cover, pay for and forgive the sins of the whole world."[2]

16. "By this we know love, because He laid down His life for us. And we also ought to lay down our lives for the brethren."

1 John 3:16 NKJV

---

[2] Stanley M. Horton, *Bible Doctrines, A Pentecostal Perspective* (Springfield, MO: Logion Press), 67.

44. WHAT ABOUT THE RESURRECTION OF JESUS? WHAT WAS THAT ALL ABOUT?

According to the Scriptures, the resurrection of Jesus was a major salvation event.

A. No one can be saved unless they believe in their heart that God raised Jesus from the dead (Romans 10:9).

B. We could not receive the gift(s) of the Holy Spirit without the resurrection (Ephesians 1:19-23, 4:8-13; Acts 2:32-33).

C. After His death, Jesus appeared to His followers as a mighty conqueror of death, hell and the grave (Revelation 1:18). We too shall conquer death and walk in a new kind of life (Romans 6:4; 1 Corinthians 15:20-23; 1 Thessalonians 4:14).

45. HOW SOLID IS THE EVIDENCE FOR THE BODILY RESURRECTION OF JESUS?

We have very good evidence that Jesus actually rose from the dead.

A. Jesus made appearances that proved that He was not a ghost (Luke 24:36-43).

B. His physical body was recognizable (John 20:14-15,26; 21:4,12).

C. Many eyewitnesses saw Him.

   (1) Mary Magdalene (Mark 16:9-11).

   (2) Other women (Matthew 28:8-10).

   (3) Peter (Luke 24:34; 1 Corinthians 15:5).

(4) The Emmaus disciples (Luke 24:1331).

(5) The ten (Luke 24:36; John 20:19).

(6) The 500 brethren (1 Corinthians 15:6).

(7) The ascension witness (Acts 1:611).

(8) The Apostle Paul (1 Corinthians 15:8).

Conclusion

Jesus Christ came to deliver the Christian (1) from God's punishment for sin; (2) from the power of sin; and (3) from the curse of the Law. Man's response is to exercise faith and repentance, and to obey the will of God (Philippians 2:12). Thus, our redemption is God's work from beginning to end.

Lesson Seven

Psalm 103:15 NLT

1. Praise the LORD, I tell myself; with my whole heart, I will praise his holy name.

2. Praise the LORD, I tell myself, and never forget the good things he does for me.

3. He forgives all my sins and heals all my diseases.

4. He ransoms me from death and surrounds me with love and tender mercies.

5. He fills my life with good things. My youth is renewed like the eagle's!

What's in It for Me?

It is a fact that whatever good there is in us (as Christians), it's there because of what God has done for us in and through Jesus Christ. We are who and what we are because of Him. Our inheritance and our identity therefore rest upon the power and provision of our heavenly Father, and not upon our individual merits. Thank God for the blood of Jesus. Thank God for the benefits that belong to us as a result of His atonement.

46. WHAT DID JESUS PURCHASE FOR US ON THE CROSS?

The Prophet Isaiah mentions four benefits that Jesus purchased for us on the cross.

A. Forgiveness of sins;

B. Deliverance from inbred iniquities;

C. Peace (inner harmony); and

D. Healing for the body.

> 5 "But he was wounded and crushed for our sins. He was beaten that we might have peace. He was whipped, and we were healed!"
>
> Isaiah 53:5 NLT

47. WHAT IS THE TRUE MEANING OF FORGIVENESS?

Hebrews 9:22 teaches us that forgiveness means that, on the basis of the shed blood of Jesus, our sins have been cancelled or removed.

> 22 "In fact, we can say that according to the law of Moses, nearly everything was purified by sprinkling with blood. Without the shedding of blood, there is no forgiveness of sins."
>
> Hebrews 9:22 NLT

48. HOW CAN WE BE SURE THAT OUR SINS HAVE BEEN FORGIVEN?

First of all, God's Word tells us that when we sin and then obey 1 John 1:9, He will forgive us and cleanse us. Secondly, the testimony of the Holy Spirit assures us that we are God's sons, i.e., we are forgiven (Romans 8:1516).

49. WHAT DOES IT MEAN TO SAY THAT WE HAVE BEEN DELIVERED FROM INBRED INIQUITIES?

Iniquities are inborn weaknesses that we have toward certain kinds of sins. These can be traced back to the sins of our ancestors (Ephesians 2:3; Romans 5:12). David said that he was shaped in iniquity and conceived in sin. This fact had a direct bearing on his moral history.

When we continue to violate God's commandments, we open the door for habits, appetites and perversions to develop in our lives (and in our children) that are abominable to God. Study the chart that follows:

The Commandment	The Iniquity
A. No other gods.	Rebellion.
B. No graven images.	Greediness and stubbornness.
C. Using God's name in vain.	Filthy/abusive conversation.

D. Keeping the Sabbath holy.   Restlessness/no peace.

E. Honoring parents.   No respect/resist authority.

F. Do not kill.   Prone to violence.

G. Do not commit adultery   Prone to sexual perversion.

H. Do not steal.   Irresistible impulse to steal.

I. Do not lie.   Deception/ dishonesty.

J. Do not covet.   Jealousy/ envy/greed.

50. HOW DID THE DEATH OF JESUS CHRIST FIGURE INTO ALL OF THIS?

The Bible teaches that through the death of Jesus, we were freed from the power and control of the sinful traits and habits that we inherited from our parents (Isaiah 53:6,10).

51. WHAT DOES THE BIBLE MEAN WHEN IT SAYS THAT JESUS WAS CHASTISED FOR OUR PEACE?

The Bible truth here is that Jesus was punished with our punishment so that we might have peace with God (Colossians 1:20).

52. WHAT IS "PEACE WITH GOD"?

"Peace with God" means "being brought back into harmony with God." When the sin problem in our lives is dealt with, then we can be on friendly terms with God.

1 "Therefore, since we have been made right in God's sight by faith, we have peace with God because of what Jesus Christ our Lord has done for us."

Romans 5:1 NLT

53. WHAT ABOUT "THE PEACE OF GOD"?

The Bible talks about "the peace of God" in Philippians 4:7. This is an inner quietness or tranquility that is brought about by the Holy Spirit inside of us (Romans 8:1516). When we really trust in God and His Word, He will give us this inner peace that will guard our hearts and minds and will keep the cares of life from destroying us.

6 "Don't worry about anything; instead, pray about everything. Tell God what you need, and thank him for all he has done. 7 If you do this, you will experience God's peace, which is far more wonderful than the human mind can understand. His peace will guard your hearts and minds as you live in Christ Jesus."

Philippians 4:67 NLT

54. WHAT ARE SOME WAYS THIS PEACE WILL AFFECT MY LIFE?

A. It will set us free from sin consciousness (Hebrews 10:22).

B. It will cleanse us from the feeling of contamination and being unfit (Romans 8:1).

C. When we die, we can stand before God knowing that everything is okay!

D. It will keep our mind sound in the hour of grief, distress and trouble (2 Timothy 1:7).

55. HOW CAN WE HOLD ON TO THIS PEACE?

The Prophet Isaiah tells us the answer to this question.

3 "You will keep in perfect peace all who trust in you, whose thoughts are fixed on you!"

Isaiah 26:3 NLT

In the midst of any circumstance in life, we can have peace that passes all understanding. This is the gift that Jesus wanted us to have. In John 14:27 He says it like this:

27 "I am leaving you with a gift — peace of mind and heart. And the peace I give isn't like the peace the world gives. So don't be troubled or afraid."

John 14:27 NLT

56. WHAT DOES THE EXPRESSION "WITH HIS STRIPES WE ARE HEALED" MEAN?

This Bible expression means that the sufferings of Jesus were used by God to provide the miracle of healing for people who are physically sick (Isaiah 53:5).

57. DOES THIS EXPRESSION REALLY REFER TO JESUS CHRIST?

We know that this expression refers to our Lord Jesus Christ, because of two New Testament passages (Matthew 8:1617; 1 Peter 2:24).

58. DOES THIS MEAN THAT EVERYONE CAN BE HEALED?

Yes! The invitation that God extends to the world is real. God wants everyone to be saved, healed and delivered.

10 "The thief's purpose is to steal and kill and destroy. My purpose is to give life in all its fullness."

John 10:10 NLT

Again . . .

9 "The Lord isn't really being slow about his promise to return, as some people think. No, he is being patient for your sake. He does not want anyone to perish, so he is giving more time for everyone to repent."

2 Peter 3:9 NLT

59. WHY IS IT THAT THERE IS STILL SO MUCH SICKNESS AND DISEASE IN THE WORLD?

This is tough to explain. For one thing, Satan is still at work in the world, and he is the source of all sickness, disease and oppression. And then, there are thousands of people who have never heard the Full Gospel message of total salvation and the abundant life. What this means is that there is a lot of doubt and unbelief in the world, and this keeps many people from God's blessings (Hosea 4:6; James 4:2).

60. HOW CAN WE BE HEALED TODAY?

Healing may be received by exercising faith in the Word of God that speaks of the provision Christ made for us at Calvary.

7 "Keep on asking, and you will be given what you ask for. Keep on looking, and you will find. Keep on knocking, and the door will be opened. 8 For everyone who asks, receives. Everyone who seeks, finds. And the door is opened to everyone who knocks. 9 You parents — if your children ask for a loaf of bread, do you give them a stone instead? 10 Or if they ask for a fish, do you give them a snake? Of course not! 11 If you sinful people know how to give good gifts to your children, how much more will your heavenly Father give good gifts to those who ask him."

Matthew 7:711 NLT

See also . . .
5 "If you need wisdom — if you want to know what God wants you to do — ask him, and he will gladly tell you. He will not resent your asking. 6 But when you ask him, be sure that you really expect him to answer, for a doubtful mind is as unsettled as a wave of the sea that is driven and tossed by the wind. 7 People like that should not expect to receive anything from the Lord. 8 They can't make up their minds. They waver back and forth in everything they do."

James 1:58 NLT

61. ARE THERE SOME OTHER WAYS FOR US TO BE HEALED?

There are several ways to receive healing:

A. Through personal prayer (James 5:16).

B. Through the ministry of the elders in the local church (James 5:1415).

C. Through the laying on of hands (Mark 16:1718).

D. Through the spoken Word (Psalm 107:20).

E. Through "aids to faith" (Acts 19:11-12).

62. WHAT ARE SOME THINGS THAT WILL BLOCK A MANIFESTATION OF HEALING? WHAT ABOUT DELAYS?

Several things should be noted here. Sometimes we forget that sin will separate us from the benefits of God. Also, unbelief is a stumbling block. Unforgiveness, unconfessed sin and the failure to make restitution can prevent us from receiving from God. Then again, a manifestation may be delayed because God wants to develop some character traits in us (patience, selfcontrol, faithfulness). Study Daniel 10 for some interesting insights into this question.

Conclusion

There are tremendous benefits available to every person who places their confidence and trust in the Lord. The Bible calls them, "The riches of grace in Christ Jesus." These are things that are divinely accomplished the moment we believe. God does the work. We receive it by faith. As you read through the New Testament, mark these scriptures that speak about your benefits in Christ.

Lesson Eight

Matthew 24:14 NLT

14 "And the Good News about the Kingdom will be preached throughout the whole world, so that all nations will hear it; and then, finally, the end will come."

Romans 1:1617 NLT

16 For I am not ashamed of this Good News about Christ. It is the power of God at work, saving everyone who believes—Jews first and also Gentiles.

17 This Good News tells us how God makes us right in his sight. This is accomplished from start to finish by faith. As the Scriptures say, "It is through faith that a righteous person has life."

Good News for Modern Man

By definition, the Gospel is "good news." It's "good news" about what God has done for us and not what we have done for Him. An important part of the purpose of God in this hour concerns the preaching or the proclamation of this Gospel. It seems that He wants to offset the popular message of "doom and gloom" with a positive word about a Kingdom of righteousness, peace and joy that's not in turmoil or strife. What's so neat about all of this is that He's going to use people like us to do the job. Think about it! God has called us to preach "good news" and to turn things around!

63. HOW IMPORTANT IS THIS SUBJECT? IN OTHER WORDS, WHAT'S THE BIG DEAL ABOUT "GOOD NEWS FOR MODERN MAN"?

The importance of this subject is really set forth in 1 Corinthians 15:12.

64. WHAT ARE SOME KEY POINTS IN THIS TEXT?

1 "Now let me remind you, dear brothers and sisters, of the Good News I preached to you before. You welcomed it then and still do now, for your faith is built on this wonderful message. 2 And it is this Good News that saves you if you firmly believe it — unless, of course, you believed something that was never true in the first place."

1 Corinthians 15:12 NLT

The first point here is that the apostles preached or proclaimed this Gospel. Secondly, common people like us welcomed or received that message and built their confidence and trust upon it. Finally, salvation was based upon this message. This makes the subject very important. It also means that our job (as preachers of the Gospel) is important.

65. IS THERE A SCRIPTURE THAT SETS FORTH THE CHRISTIAN GOSPEL IN A CLEAR AND BRIEF FASHION?

Actually there is such a scripture. It's found in Ephesians 2:1-10.

1 "As for you, you were dead in your transgressions and sins, 2 in which you used to live when you followed the ways of this world and of the ruler of the kingdom of the air, the spirit who is now at work in those who are disobedient. 3 All of us also lived among them at one time, gratifying the cravings of our sinful nature and following its desires and thoughts. Like the rest, we were by nature objects of wrath. 4 But because of his great love for us, God, who is rich in mercy, 5 made us alive with Christ even when we were dead in transgressions — it is by grace you have been saved. 6 And God raised us up with Christ and seated us with him in the heavenly realms in Christ Jesus, 7 in order that in the coming ages he might show the incomparable riches of his grace, expressed in his kindness to us in Christ Jesus. 8 For it is by grace you have been saved, through faith — and this not from yourselves, it is the gift of God — 9 not by works, so that no one can boast. 10 For we are God's workmanship, created in Christ Jesus to do good works, which God prepared in advance for us to do."

Ephesians 2:110 NIV

Note! In this text, we are given reliable and accurate information that can be used to set us free from sin and its consequences.

66. WHAT IS THE THREEFOLD BREAKDOWN OF THIS PASSAGE?

This passage is filled with spiritual truth. The first three verses reveal important truths about ourselves. Verses 4 through 7 tell us about the One True God. The last three verses reveal the heart of New Covenant salvation.

67. WHAT DOES THIS TEXT REVEAL ABOUT OURSELVES?

The truth revealed here is not "good news." Outside of Jesus Christ, the Bible says that we are dead — "doomed forever because of our many sins." Spiritually speaking, we are lifeless, helpless and hopeless. We are separated from God's life and disconnected from His power. The truth revealed here is that all people are in the same boat. The apostle says the same thing in Romans 3:912.

> 9 "Well then, are we Jews better than others? No, not at all, for we have already shown that all people, whether Jews or Gentiles, are under the power of sin. 10 As the Scriptures say, 'No one is good — not even one. 11 No one has real understanding; no one is seeking God. 12 All have turned away from God; all have gone wrong. No one does good, not even one.'"

Romans 3:912 NLT

This first section of the text concludes with the devastating words of verse 3.

3 "True, some of them were unfaithful; but just because they broke their promises, does that mean God will break his promises?"

Romans 3:3 NLT

The point here is quite clear. Our condition, apart from Jesus Christ, is desperate. Sin, death and wrath are our common experiences. We are spiritually destitute and are justly condemned by a holy God.

68. WHAT ARE WE TAUGHT IN EPHESIANS 2:4-7 ABOUT THE ONE TRUE GOD?

A. In verse 4 we are taught that the one true God has "great love for us" and is "rich in mercy." This is the picture of God that we must hold on to. To be involved with Him is to be involved with boundless love and mercy.

B. In verses 5 and 6 we are told what this loving and merciful God did for us (believers). First of all, He "made us alive with Christ." Secondly, He "raised us up together" with Christ. Thirdly, He "seated us, or enthroned us, in the heavenly realms in Christ Jesus." Basically, we are here given three definite ways in which our loving and merciful God expressed Himself.

These are love expressions that impacted everything.

C. If the question is ever raised as to why this loving God acted as He did, the answer is clear and simple:

7 "In order that in the coming ages he might show the incomparable riches of his grace, expressed in his kindness to us in Christ Jesus."

Ephesians 2:7 NIV

Note! Someone has said that what God wanted to do was to have us as trophies of His grace. He intends to show us to the universe as prime examples of love and mercy.

69. WHAT ABOUT NEW COVENANT SALVATION? WHAT DOES THIS "GOSPEL MESSAGE" REVEAL ABOUT BEING SAVED?

This last section of the text (vv. 8-10) teaches that New Covenant salvation is completely "by grace" and "through faith." All of this is to say that we cannot take credit for our salvation. Why? Because our salvation is a gift from God.

We also learn that God's intention in saving us is so that we might perform the good works that He had planned for us long ago.

Foundation Stones

Section Three

GOALS AND OBJECTIVES

- To come to a saving knowledge of the truth
- To "properly" lay the foundation stones in our lives
- To know for a certainty those things in which we've been instructed
- To be rooted and built up in Him and established in the faith

Many people today would lead us to believe that it doesn't matter what you believe so long as you've accepted Christ as your Savior. The scriptures, however, emphatically refute this. First Peter 3:15 says,

> *"Sanctify the Lord God in your hearts and always be ready to give a defense to anyone who asks you a reason for the hope that is in you, with meekness and fear."*

All who would "be no more children, tossed to and fro and carried away with every wind of doctrine, by the trickery of men in the cunning craftiness of deceitful plotting" must become firmly established in the apostles doctrine and fellowship. For this there is no substitution.

Lesson Nine

Matthew 3:1-12

1 In those days came John the Baptist, preaching in the wilderness of Judaea,

2 And saying, Repent ye: for the kingdom of heaven is at hand.

3 For this is he that was spoken of by the prophet Esaias, saying, The voice of one crying in the wilderness, Prepare ye the way of the Lord, make his paths straight.

4 And the same John had his raiment of camel's hair, and a leathern girdle about his loins; and his meat was locusts and wild honey.

5 Then went out to him Jerusalem, and all Judaea, and all the region round about Jordan,

6 And were baptized of him in Jordan, confessing their sins.

7 But when he saw many of the Pharisees and Sadducees come to his baptism, he said unto them, O generation of vipers, who hath warned you to flee from the wrath to come?

8 Bring forth therefore fruits meet for repentance:

9 And think not to say within yourselves, We have Abraham to our father: for I say unto you, that God is able of these stones to raise up children unto Abraham.

10 And now also the axe is laid unto the root of the trees: therefore every tree which bringeth not forth good fruit is hewn down, and cast into the fire.

11 I indeed baptize you with water unto repentance: but he that cometh after me is mightier than I, whose shoes I am not worthy to bear: he shall baptize you with the Holy Ghost, and with fire:

12 Whose fan is in his hand, and he will throughly purge his floor, and gather his wheat into the garner; but he will burn up the chaff with unquenchable fire.

Repentance From Dead Works

Repentance from dead works is the first step toward entering the Kingdom of God.

70. WHAT DOES THE WORD REPENTANCE MEAN?

A. One Old Testament word, "NACHAM" means to grieve or to lament.

B. Another Old Testament word, "SHUBH" means a radical change in one's attitude toward sin and God.

C. The main New Testament word for repentance, "METANOEO" means to have another mind; it refers to a change of mind that follows consideration and regret. It involves a change of direction and action [cp. Mt. 21:28-31; 3:1-10; Lk 3:9-14].

71. WHAT ARE THE "DEAD WORKS" REFERRED TO IN HEBREWS 6:1 AND HEBREWS 9:14?

The "Dead Works" referred to in the above Scriptures are those works which pertain to the "Old Man" [1 Cor. 15:22]. They both deserve and express death in trespasses and sins. These are also called "Works of the flesh" [cp. Gal. 5:19-21; Col. 3:5-10; I Cor. 6:9-11].

Dead Works are moreover those man-made rites, customs, belief, and rituals that we perform believing that they will earn us an entrance into God's Kingdom. These are based upon

"Dead tradition" rather than revelation or the Word of God. They are really futile attempts to work out our own salvation hoping that God will approve [cp. Col. 2:8, 16, 20-23 (Amp.); Tit. 3:5]. See the story of the Tower of Babel in Genesis 11:1ff.

72. WHAT DOES EPHESIANS 2:8-10 TEACH US IN THIS RESPECT?

Here we learn that we who have been resurrected from "death in sins" are the handiwork of God, and have been created in Christ Jesus unto "good works" and not "dead works." This being the case then, it's all the more necessary that we turn away from dead traditions because:

A. They destroy and nullify real worship and praise [Mt. 15:3-9].

B. They make the true Word of God ineffective, vain and fruitless [cp. Mk. 7:1-13; Mt. 23].

C. They are a stumbling block to new Christians [Gal. 1:11 "… not after man."].

73. HOW IMPORTANT IS IT THAT ONE ACKNOWLEDGE THE NEED TO REPENT?

Simply put, until one is ready to change, they are not prepared to do business with God [cp. Prov. 14:12; Rom. 3:9-23].

74. THE KIND OF CHANGE THAT'S ASSOCIATED WITH REAL REPENTANCE IS CAUSED BY AT LEAST THREE THINGS. WHAT ARE THEY?

A. The preaching of the Word [cp. Ps. 119:130; Heb. 4:12; Acts 2:37].

B. Rebuke [cp. II Cor. 7:8-10; Prov. 27:5; Titus 1:13].

C. Studying the Scriptures [cp. Acts 17:11; II Tim. 3:15-17].

75. **DOES THE BIBLE TEACH THAT REPENTANCE IS A GIFT?**

Yes! The Scriptures clearly shows that repentance is a gift from God [cp. Acts 5:31, 11:18; II Tim. 2:24-25].

76. **WHY IS IT THAT SOME PEOPLE CAN RECEIVE THE GIFT OF REPENTANCE WHILE OTHERS DO NOT?**

The willingness to forgive others plays a part in God granting repentance [cp. Heb. 12:14-17; Mt. 5:7, 6:14-15, 21-35].

77. **WHAT ARE SOME EVIDENCES OF REAL REPENTANCE?**

A. Read Psalms 34:18; 51:16 and Isaiah 66:2.

B. Read Isaiah 53:6; 55:6-8; Acts 2:27-41, and II Cor. 7:8-11.

Conclusion

Repentance is really acknowledging that our ways are wrong and that they lead to death. Repentance also involves making a radical change in our thoughts and our behavior. As such, repentance is the first step to new life in the Kingdom of God.

Note! The Process of repentance is four fold:

- Consideration of our ways
- Sorrow for transgression

- Renunciation of old ways
- Change of behavior

Lesson Ten

Hebrews 11:1-6

1 Now faith is the substance of things hoped for, the evidence of things not seen.

2 For by it the elders obtained a good report.

3 Through faith we understand that the worlds were framed by the word of God, so that things which are seen were not made of things which do appear.

4 By faith Abel offered unto God a more excellent sacrifice than Cain, by which he obtained witness that he was righteous, God testifying of his gifts: and by it he being dead yet speaketh.

5 By faith Enoch was translated that he should not see death; and was not found, because God had translated him: for before his translation he had this testimony, that he pleased God.

6 But without faith it is impossible to please him: for he that cometh to God must believe that he is, and that he is a rewarder of them that diligently seek him.

FAITH TOWARD GOD

Faith is fundamental in the ministry of Jesus Christ as well as in the creed and conduct of the New Testament Church. For instance, in the stories of the Syrophonecian woman, the Centurion and blind Bartimaeus, Jesus saw and rewarded their faith, and in so doing He established confidence and trust in God as the paramount virtue in the Kingdom.

78. WHAT DOES THE WORD "FAITH" MEAN?

The best definition available to us is probably that in *Webster's New World Dictionary of the American Language*. Faith is there defined as: "Unquestioning, complete, confidence and trust in God."

79. WHAT IS A GOOD PARAPHRASE OF THE BIBLICAL DEFINITION OF FAITH AS GIVEN IN HEBREWS 11:1?

Faith is right now the substance (or spiritual stuff)which stands under and gives support and foundation to "hoped for things." Faith is moreover the absolute proof of the reality of things that cannot be seen touched, heard, smelled or tasted.

The Scriptures presuppose the existence of two worlds [cp. II Cor. 4:16-18; Heb. 11:27]. Faith concerns the invisible realm of God and is related to "things hoped for" [Mk. 11:24] and "things not seen." In the invisible realm of God, this substance called faith is just as real as any material substance in the visible realm of sense experience.

80. WHAT ARE THE THREE ELEMENTS IN THE GENERAL SENSE OF THE WORD "FAITH?"

A. Knowledge

Faith is not a blind leap into the dark, nor is it believing something without any evidence. To the contrary, faith rests upon the solid evidence of the Word or revelation of God. This being the case, any real act of faith presupposes knowlege of the truth of the living word of God [cp. Ps. 9:10; Jn. 9:35-38; Rom. 10:17].

B. Spiritual Assent

It's not enough just to have "head knowledge" of the ability of the Lord Jesus Christ to save, heal and deliver; there must be also an assent (compliance, agreement, "yes - saying") of the heart or spirit to the claims of Christ that are unveiled in the Word [cp. Jn. 10:30, 14:6, 9-14, 16:24-30]. In the New Testament, Jesus Christ is revealed to be:

- Our High Priest
- Our Shepherd
- Our Life
- Our Lord and Savior
- Our Deliverer
- Our Healer
- The Baptizer in the Holy Spirit
- The Truth, The Way and The Life
- Our Intercessor

C. Appropriation

The "realities" that have been revealed to us in the Scriptures and assented to in our hearts must be personally "taken hold of" by acting on the Word; i.e., consenting to Christ Jesus [cp. Jn. 1:12; 5:24].

81. HOW ARE WE TO UNDERSTAND THE SOURCE OF FAITH?

Real faith has its source in God. It is born out of our relationship with God. More specifically, faith (insofar as it is a firm conviction or persuasion existing in the heart or spirit of the Christian as a spiritual substance) comes forth and is formed in the heart as a result of hearing the "Rhema" of God. That such a "Rhema" has indeed been heard and received will be evidenced by corresponding actions.

Study these Scriptures: Hebrews 12:2; Romans 10:17; 4:17; and 5:1.

82. HOW ARE WE TO UNDERSTAND THE RELATIONSHIP BETWEEN FAITH AND REPENTANCE?

Faith and repentance are flip sides of the one authentic or proper response of man to the Word of God. When a man properly responds to God's Word, he will, according to I Thessalonians 1:9, "Turn to God" (faith) and "Turn from idols" (repentance). Real conversion necessitates both of these aspects.

83. HOW IS FAITH USED WITH RESPECT TO NEW COVENANT PRAYER?

I John 5:14-15, James 1:5-7, and Mark 11:24 should be studied in this connection. It's important to understand thoroughly the promises upon which our prayer or petition is based.

Next, we must believe that those promises are worth their full face value. We must believe, in other words, that God said what He meant and meant what he said. Thirdly, we've got to act like God told us the truth. We've got to step out on God's Word with great boldness and importunity even though at the moment our sense experience is contrary to the revelation of the Scriptures.

84. WHAT IS THE UNIQUE AND SUPREME VALUE OF "FAITH TOWARD GOD?"

A. It is the only God-ordained way of justification or righteousness [cp. Rom. 3:22, 25,28,30,4:5, 5:1; Gal. 3:8,24].

B. It is the way to receive the promises of God.

Observe!

(1) All born again believers are recipients of a vast and tremendous inheritance [l Pet. 1:34; Rom. 8:16-17; II Cor. 3:21:23].

(2) Five conditions of faith must be met in order to draw on this inheritance.

- Ground your faith in the Word of God.
- Claim as yours what your faith has embraced from the Word of God.
- Boldly confess what you believe you received by faith [Mk. 11:24].
- Act in harmony with your faith.
- Hold fast our confession of faith without wavering.

C. It is the way of life that becomes the righteous [cp. Hab. 2:4; Rom. 1:17; Gal. 3:11; Heb. 10:38].

The Word "live" in the above references envision all of the activities of which life consists: walking, eating, sleeping, working, praying, fighting, etc.

D. It is the one thing necessary to pleasing God [Heb. 11:6].

85. HOW MUST WE UNDERSTAND THE RELATIONSHIP BETWEEN FAITH AND WORKS?

The only faith that "saves," "heals," and "delivers" is faith in the Lord Jesus Christ. Faith in any other savior will not work. Faith in any other gospel will not do the job [Gal. 1:8-9].

As far as works are concerned, the Scriptures clearly teach that we are "set right" in the sight of God on a non-merit basis. We are, in other words, justified without any works on our part whatsoever! The Apostle James however (see James 2:14-26) teaches that our righteous standing before God will be evidenced or demonstrated by good works or corresponding actions. He makes the point that, "Faith that does not result in good deeds IS NOT REAL FAITH." We conclude then that there is no contradiction between Paul and James. They are actually complimenting each other. Heart faith brings us salvation; active obedience to the Word of God demonstrates the genuineness of our trust.

Conclusion

Faith is trusting God so that a relationship with Him can be established. It is in this living relationship (based upon confidence and trust in God's faithfulness) that we learn His ways. Obviously, cultivating an authentic living relationship with

God is more important than trying to work a "success formula." God is pleased when we trust in Him with all our hearts and refuse to put confidence in our own understanding.

Lesson Eleven

Romans 6:3-7

3 Know ye not, that so many of us as were baptized into Jesus Christ were baptized into his death?

4 Therefore we are buried with him by baptism into death: that like as Christ was raised up from the dead by the glory of the Father, even so we also should walk in newness of life.

5 For if we have been planted together in the likeness of his death, we shall be also in the likeness of his resurrection:

6 Knowing this, that our old man is crucified with him, that the body of sin might be destroyed, that henceforth we should not serve sin.

7 For he that is dead is freed from sin.

1 Corinthians 12:13

13 For by one Spirit are we all baptized into one body, whether we be Jews or Gentiles, whether we be bond or free; and have been all made to drink into one Spirit.

Galatians 3:27

27 For as many of you as have been baptized into Christ have put on Christ.

The Doctrine of Baptisms: Into the Body of Christ

Three baptisms pertain to the New Covenant and the Christian believer: Baptism into the Body of Christ; Baptism in Water, and Baptism into the Holy Spirit. These baptisms (along with Repentance from Dead Works and Faith Toward God) constitute an entrance into Kingdom life.

86. WHAT DOES THE WORD "BAPTIZE" MEAN?

A. To plunge into

B. To introduce into

C. To overwhelm

D. To submerge

E. To immerse

F. To thrust under

87. WHAT IS THE BODY OF CHRIST?

The Body of Christ is one of several New Testament designations for the Church universal; i.e., the whole company of born again believers gathered during the Dispensation of Grace. Essentially, the "Body of Christ" and the "Spiritual Kingdom of God" are the same. To be in the one, is equivalent to being in the other [cp. Col. 1:18, 24; I Cor. 12:27-28; Mt. 16:17-19].

88. WHAT IS IT TO BE BAPTIZED INTO THE BODY OF CHRIST?

Baptism into the Body of Christ means to be introduced into the Kingdom of God. This immersion is moreover called the "New Birth" or being "Born from above." Sometimes this baptism, "of which" the Holy Spirit is the administrator, is confused with the Baptism in the Holy Spirit. The following Scriptures clarify the issue: John 3:3, 5-6; Galatians 3:27; Titus 3:5; and I Peter 1:23.

89. MORE SPECIFICALLY, WHAT HAPPENS WHEN WE ARE "BORN AGAIN?"

A. We are "made alive" in the "inner man" [cp. Eph. 2:1, 5: II Cor. 5:17; Jn. 3:4,6].

B. We receive of the "fullness of God" [cp. Jn. 1:16; Col. 1:19, 2:3, 9, 10; Pet. 1:3-4].

C. "Old Things" pass away [cp. Col. 2:9-13: II Cor. 5:17; Rom. 8:1-2; Eph. 2:1-3, 8-13].

D. We are "joined to Christ" [cp. I Cor. 6:17, 12:27; Jn. 15:1ff; Acts 2:47].

E. We are joined to other members of the Body [cp. Eph. 4:25; Rom. 12:5].

90. WHAT ARE SOME BIBLICAL STEPS THAT ONE CAN TAKE THAT WILL RESULT IN BEING BAPTIZED INTO THE BODY OF CHRIST?

A. Come to Jesus in accordance with John 6:37.

B. Call upon the Lord to save you. [Rom. 10:13]

C. Obey Romans 10:9-10.

D. Obey Acts 2:37-38.

Study carefully I John 5:1; I Corinthians 12:13, and Romans 6:3-7.

Conclusion

The Spiritual realm or sphere in which "born again" believers live their lives is called "The Body of Christ." Here we are joined to the Lord Jesus Christ and other true believers in a spiritual union of life wherein we will never perish. Being in the Body of Christ is what qualifies us for the baptism in the Holy Spirit. It is the Universal, Spiritual Kingdom of God.

Lesson Twelve

Acts 2:38-41

38 Then Peter said unto them, Repent, and be baptized every one of you in the name of Jesus Christ for the remission of sins, and ye shall receive the gift of the Holy Ghost.

39 For the promise is unto you, and to your children, and to all that are afar off, even as many as the Lord our God shall call.

40 And with many other words did he testify and exhort, saying, Save yourselves from this untoward generation.

41 Then they that gladly received his word were baptized: and the same day there were added unto them about three thousand souls.

The Doctrine of Baptisms: Into Water

New Covenant baptism in water is more than a routine tradition or custom. Actually, water baptism bespeaks of the believer's basic identification with Christ in His death, burial, and resurrection. Moreover, through immersion in water, the obedient candidate testifies to the Lordship of Jesus Christ, a Lordship or Government into which he has entered and to which he has submitted by faith.

91. WHAT GAVE RISE TO THE QUESTION STATED IN ACTS 2:37B?

When the "men of Israel" heard the provoking word about the Lordship of Jesus Christ, they were "pricked in their hearts" and frantically inquired, "What shall we do?"

92. WHY DID PETER INSTRUCT NEW CONVERTS TO BE "BAPTIZED EVERYONE OF YOU IN THE NAME OF JESUS CHRIST?"

A. Because "The Lord Jesus Christ" is the name of God in the New Covenant [cp. Col. 1:19, 2-9].

B. Because our Lord had commission that disciples were to be baptized "in the Name of the Father and of the Son and of the Holy Ghost."

C. In view of John 16:12-13 and John 14:26, Peter was giving clear proof that the promised revelation of Jesus

Christ via the Holy Spirit had been received. He was simply acting upon newly given "revelation knowledge."

D. He was complying with a God-given precedent which circulated in the apostolic fellowship and the New Covenant Community.

93. HOW IS BAPTISM IN WATER RELATED TO "THE REMISSION OF SINS?"

The term "Remission of Sins" may be stated as the "forgiveness of sins." Remission means "to forgive"; "to send off and away;" "to separate from."

A. The Bible teaches that Jesus provides "forgiveness of sins" [Acts 5:31].

B. Forgiveness or Remission of sins is based upon the shed blood of Jesus. It is important to see here that forgiveness always follows the execution of penalty. Without this, there can be NO remission of sins [cp. Lev. 4:35; Mt. 26:28; Heb. 9:22, I Jn. 1:6-9, 2:2].

C. Faith is essential to receiving forgiveness [Acts 10:43].

D. Acts 2:38 is perhaps better translated, "Be baptized every one of you because of the remission or forgiveness of sins." The key here is to see that the Greek preposition, "EIS" (KJV says, "for") really indicates the basis upon which forgiveness is granted and not the aim or purpose of the sacrament of Water Baptism. The remission of sins is based upon the shed blood of Jesus and is received by faith. The fact of this remission is the basis for being baptized in water. To summarize then, Water Baptism rather than causing sins to be "sent off and away" gives visible expression to the faith by and through which forgiveness has been received. Such forgiveness or remission of sins is (according to the clear testimony of the Scriptures) based upon the shed blood of Jesus Christ alone.

94. WHAT HAS WATER BAPTISM TO DO WITH CLEANSING? [CP. ACTS 22:16; REV. 1:5; JN. 15:3]

Two aspects of cleansing should be noted in this connection. First, Jesus Christ washes us from our sins legally by His Blood. Secondly, we are cleansed by the Word of God experimentally, as we "take heed thereto." [Ps. 119:9] In this light, Water Baptism signifies and "makes real in our experience" the great purpose of the Father God in washing us and in saving us from our sins. [cp. Eph. 5:26-27; Jude 24]

95. HOW IS WATER BAPTISM RELATED TO CIRCUMCISION?

What the circumcision of the flesh was in the Old Covenant, the circumcision of the heart is to the New Covenant. First of all, it is an initiation into the covenant. See Genesis 17:9-14. Secondly, circumcision is a sign or seal of faith. Although Abraham was justified by faith, He carried in his body a mark, a personal reminder of his relationship to God. This same principle is found in the New Covenant. We are justified by faith and we receive the circumcision of heart in water baptism (Rom. 4:11). Finally, by circumcision of heart we are set apart unto God as His purchased possession (Gal. 6:15-16 with Rom. 2:28-29).

96. READ COLOSSIANS 2:9-14 IN THE AMPLIFIED BIBLE. UNDER THE NEW COVENANT, IS

SOMETHING SPIRITUAL REMOVED FROM US IN THE WATERS OF BAPTISM?

The thing that is removed from us in water baptism is called "the old man" or "the body of sin." This is what we bury. This is when the enmity between us and God comes to an end.

97. SHOULD INFANTS BE BAPTIZED IN WATER?

Observe!

In the Scriptures, there are absolutely no grounds for infant water baptism.

A. Nevertheless, those who argue for infant baptism rightfully take baptism as a substitute for circumcism, which was done when Israelite boy babies were eight days old. However, when the New Testament deals with circumcision it clearly has in view a knowledgeable believer who has prepared his or her heart through repentance and faith (Dt. 30:6; Ezk. 11:19-20; Acts 2:38).

B. Because the Bible says that the promise is "for you and your children" and because Paul baptized the household of Stephanas, some take this to point to infant baptism. But in those days, children were not considered full members of the household until the time of their "adoption". (Acts 2:39; I Cor. 1:16).

C. Peter commanded the people to "repent and be baptized". Infants are incapable of repentance, faith, and public testimony to salvation. In fact they have no sins for which to repent. Does this mean that infants and children who die before the age of accountability are still saved through the redemption that is provided by Christ Jesus? The answer is, "yes".

It's important to see here that principle of family solidarity in the covenant community is at the heart of the Christian life. In I Corinthians 7:13-14 we learn that unsaved marriage partners and infants are set apart unto God, and share covenant status with the saved marriage partner (parent) in a special kind of way. Infants in this situation should be dedicated to God; brought up to live for the Lord and led to the point of personal faith and baptism in the name of the Lord. After this they can enjoy full covenant status and life. We believe that if infants of saved parents die before the age of accountability they will be saved.

"Jesus called the children to him and said, "let the little children come to me, and do not hinder them, for the kingdom of God belongs to such as these."

Luke 18:16 (NIV)

98. WHEN SHOULD CANDIDATES BE BAPTIZED?

Scriptural evidence indicates that water baptism should take place as soon as possible after being born-again and introduced into the Body of Christ.

- A. The Ethiopian eunuch was baptized immediately upon his decision to follow Christ (Acts 8:36-38).

- B. Cornelius and his friends were baptized the same day as their conversion (Acts 10:44-48).

- C. Lydia and her household were baptized right after their conversion (Acts 16:14-15).

D. The Philippian jailer and his household were baptized the same night of their conversion (Acts 16:30-33).

Conclusion

Thus we see that, New Covenant water baptism is more than a routine tradition or custom. It is more than an outward sign of an inward grace. Actually, water baptism has to do with the basic identification of the believer. It speaks of his death, burial, and resurrection. Moreover, through public immersion in water, the believer testifies to the Lordship of Jesus Christ to which he or she has submitted by faith.

Lesson Thirteen

Acts 1:5,8

5 For John truly baptized with water; but ye shall be baptized with the Holy Ghost not many days hence.

8 But ye shall receive power, after that the Holy Ghost is come upon you: and ye shall be witnesses unto me both in Jerusalem, and in all Judaea, and in Samaria, and unto the uttermost part of the earth.

Acts 2:1-4

1 And when the day of Pentecost was fully come, they were all with one accord in one place.

2 And suddenly there came a sound from heaven as of a rushing mighty wind, and it filled all the house where they were sitting.

3 And there appeared unto them cloven tongues like as of fire, and it sat upon each of them.

4 And they were all filled with the Holy Ghost, and began to speak with other tongues, as the Spirit gave them utterance.

Acts 19:2-3

2   He said unto them, Have ye received the Holy Ghost since ye believed? And they said unto him, We have not so much as heard whether there be any Holy Ghost.

3   And he said unto them, Unto what then were ye baptized? And they said, Unto John's baptism.

THE DOCTRINE OF BAPTISMS: INTO THE HOLY SPIRIT

"All believers are entitled to, and should ardently expect, and earnestly seek the promise of the Father, the Baptism in the Holy Ghost and fire, according to the command of our Lord Jesus Christ. This was the normal experience of all in the early Christian church. With it comes the enduement of power for life and service, the bestowment of the gifts and their uses in the work of the ministry (Lk 24:49; Acts 1:4,8; I Cor. 12:1-15).[1]

This statement of faith was later expanded with the following addition:

"This experience is distinct from and subsequent to the experience of the New Birth (Acts 8:12-17; 10:44-46; 11:14-16; 15:7-9). With the Baptism in the Holy Ghost come such experiences as an overflowing fullness of the Spirit (John 7:37-38; Acts 4:8); an intensified consecration to God and dedication to His work (Acts 2:43; Heb. 12:28); and a more active love for Christ, for His Word and for the lost (Mark 16:20).[2]

All who believe the Scriptures will wholeheartedly agree with this declaration of faith.

99. WHAT ARE SOME OF THE MINISTRIES OF THE HOLY SPIRIT OF GOD?

A. The Holy Spirit reproves or convicts the world of sin, righteousness and judgment (Jn. 16:8-11).

B. The regeneration of the believer is a ministry of the Holy Spirit (Jn. 3:6).

C. Placing believers into the Spiritual Kingdom of God is a ministry of the Holy Spirit (1 Cor. 12:13).

D. The Holy Spirit stamps or seals the believer with His divine presence and thus confirms or authenticates the believers' standing or position in Christ (Eph. 4:30; II Cor. 1:22; Eph. 1:13).

100. WHAT IS THE BAPTISM IN THE HOLY SPIRIT?

The Baptism in the Holy Spirit is a supernatural enduement with power from on high (Jn. 1:33). It is a seal of God's work within us. This baptism is moreover a complete immersion of believers in the Holy Spirit thus granting to them access into the realm of God's supernatural power and ability (Acts 1:8; Jn. 14:12; I Cor. 2:4; Gal. 5:22-25; Col. 3:5-10; I Cor. 6:9-11).

101. HOW MUST WE UNDERSTAND THE OUTWARD ASPECT OF THE EXPERIENCE OF BEING BAPTIZED IN THE SPIRIT?

In this outward aspect of the experience, the Holy Spirit is depicted as being " poured out " upon believers.(Acts 10:45).

Therefore being by the right hand of God exalted, and having received of the Father the promise of the Holy Ghost, he hath <u>shed forth</u> this, which ye now see and hear.

Acts 2:33

And as I began to speak, <u>the Holy ghost fell on</u> them, as on us at the beginning.

Acts 11:15

And when Paul had laid his hands upon them, <u>the Holy Ghost came</u> on them; and they spake with tongues, and prophesied.

Acts 19:6

102. WHAT ABOUT THE INWARD ASPECT OF BEING BAPTIZED IN THE HOLY SPIRIT?

In this aspect, the believer (in the likeness of someone drinking in water) receives the presence and power of the Spirit of God within himself until the Spirit thus received wells up within the believer and then flows out like rivers from his innermost being (Jn. 7:37-39).

103. WHO CAN RECEIVE THE BAPTISM IN THE HOLY SPIRIT?

The promise of the Father was given to disciples who were already in close communion with Christ. Their names were already written in heaven. They were clean before God, having had a spiritual bath through the truth. In a word, only those who have been introduced into the Body of Christ can receive the Baptism in the Holy Spirit. In other words, this experience is only for those who have been "made alive in the inner man", "joined to Christ in the spirit", and "translated out of the dominion of darkness and transferred into the Kingdom of His beloved son".

104. HOW DOES THE BAPTISM IN THE HOLY SPIRIT HELP AND STRENGTHEN THE LIFE OF THE BELIEVER?

A. The Holy Spirit gives and provides the ability to minister effectively (Acts 1:8).

B. The Baptism in the Holy Spirit is the doorway leading into a mode of worship that blesses the Lord and His saints (Jn. 4:24; Phil. 3:3; Heb. 2:12).

C. The Baptism in the Holy Spirit gives added power in prayer (Rom. 8:26-27; Jude 20).

D. The Baptism in the Holy Spirit opens the door for "revelation knowledge" and understanding of the Scriptures (I Cor. 2:12; Jn. 16:13).

E. The Baptism in the Holy Spirit enables us to hear (more accurately) the voice of the Lord and to receive guidance and direction thereby (Acts 13:1-2; Mk. 13:11; Acts 1:2).

The Baptism in the Holy Spirit opens the way for the exercise of spiritual gifts to the glory of God and the strengthening of the ministry.

105. WHAT OUTWARD MANIFESTATION ACCOMPANIES THE INWARD EXPERIENCE OF BEING "BAPTIZED IN" OR "FILLED WITH" THE HOLY SPIRIT?

Full Gospel Baptist's teach, for the most part, that the manifestation of speaking in tongues is an initial evidence of Spirit Baptism. National and Progressive Baptist's tend to disagree with them on this point. Neither the National Baptist Convention USA, Inc. nor the Progressive National Baptist Convention make a doctrinal statement on "The Baptism in The Holy Spirit."

This catechism reflects more of a Full Gospel Baptist perspective, likened to that of Bishop Andy C. Lewter, who writes:

So the Full Gospel Baptist Church Fellowship is just that, a Fellowship of Baptist churches with Holiness beliefs and concerns about the life of sanctification. They worship in a manner often associated with Pentecostals; but, they are distinctly not Pentecostal in their beliefs about the church. For instance, Full Gospel Baptist's have bishops, but those bishops do not have any vested authority over churches. Rather, the bishops and the Full Gospel Baptist Church Fellowship exist to serve.

Because all Baptist churches are autonomous bodies, they must study Acts 2:1-4; 4:31; 8:14-17; 9:17; 10:44-46; 19:1-6 and formulate their own position statement that is consistent with The Word Of God.

106. WHAT SPIRITUAL TRUTH DO YOU SEE IN THE SCRIPTURES BELOW ?

    A. I Corinthians 14:2,4,14

    B. John 14:16 -17

    C. Romans 8:26-27

    D. Jude 20

    E. I Corinthians 14:14

    NOTE! READ THESE VERSES IN THREE DIFFERENT TRANSLATIONS

107. HOW DOES A BELIEVER RECEIVE THE BAPTISM IN THE HOLY SPIRIT?

  A. Heart Preparation

- Believe and confess that the Bible teaches that the Baptism in the Holy Spirit is a personal experience after salvation and is promised to all believers (Joel 2:28; Acts 1:4-5,8; 2:1ff; 2:38; Lk. 11:9-13).
- Recognize your need for the Baptism in the Holy Spirit.
- Expect to receive with all your heart.
- Be willing to receive the Baptism in the Holy Spirit on God's terms.

B. The Act of Faith

- Believe God's Word which promised you the Holy Spirit (Acts 2:38-39; 10:45).
- Ask in Faith for the Baptism in the Holy Spirit (Lk. 11:9-13).
- Confess that you have received the Holy Spirit by faith (Mk. 11:24).
- Illustration: "Heavenly Father, based upon Your Word of promise, I now ask for, and by faith receive, the gift of the Holy Spirit, in Jesus' Name.
- Act on your Faith.

Conclusion

There is a difference between being born of the Spirit and being baptized in the Spirit. When a true believer is born of the Spirit, he or she becomes a partaker of the nature of God and receives of the fullness of God. According to I Corinthians 6:17, born again believers are also joined to Christ in a vital union of life. In this way, the problem of spiritual death is resolved. The Bible teaches that this work of the Holy Spirit is followed by the Pentecostal outpouring referred to as being filled with the Spirit, or baptized in the Spirit.

Lesson Fourteen

Numbers 27:15-20

15 And Moses spake unto the Lord, saying,

16 Let the Lord, the God of the spirits of all flesh, set a man over the congregation,

17 Which may go out before them, and which may go in before them, and which may lead them out, and which may bring them in; that the congregation of the Lord be not as sheep which have no shepherd.

18 And the Lord said unto Moses, Take thee Joshua the son of Nun, a man in whom is the spirit, and lay thine hand upon him;

19 And set him before Eleazar the priest, and before all the congregation; and give him a charge in their sight.

20 And thou shalt put some of thine honour upon him, that all the congregation of the children of Israel may be obedient.

I Timothy 4:12-14

12 Let no man despise thy youth; but be thou an example of the believers, in word, in conversation, in charity, in spirit, in faith, in purity.

13 Till I come, give attendance to reading, to exhortation, to doctrine.

14 Neglect not the gift that is in thee, which was given thee by prophecy, with the laying on of the hands of the presbytery.

THE LAYING ON OF HANDS

The doctrine of the "Laying on of Hands" is the fourth foundational principle listed in Hebrews 6:1-2. This doctrine depicts an act in which one person lays his hands upon another person, thus signifying Transference, Transmission, Impartation, and Identification.

More specifically, "The Laying on of Hands" emphasizes the truth that through the Law of Contact and Transmission what is in or at the disposal of one person may be passed on or imparted to another person. This truth is given throughout the Scriptures of the Old and New Testaments.

108. WHAT PART DID "LAYING ON OF HANDS" PLAY IN THE OLD TESTAMENT?

A. The Patriarch Jacob laid his hands upon his grandchildren and pronounced blessings upon them (Gen. 48:8-20).

B. The Lord God obligated each Israelite to offer an animal sacrifice. Just before the killing of the animal, the Israelite laid his hand on the head of the animal thereby transferring his sins to the sacrifice. This symbolic act was followed throughout Old Testament time (Lev. 1:4, 3:2; 16:21-22).

C. Moses, through the "Laying on of Hands" with respect to Joshua, accomplished two things:

- He passed some of his honor onto Joshua.

- He publicly acknowledged that God had indeed appointed Joshua as the next leader over Israel (Num. 27:15-23; Dt. 31:7-8; 34:9).

D. Elijah imparted to Elisha "a double portion" of his spirit based on the Law of Contact and Transmission (Acts 19:11-12; 1 Kgs. 19:13-21; II Kgs. 2:9-14).

Note!

The "Laying on of Hands" is not directly involved, but the Law governing the Ordinance is. Observe the importance of contact with the mantle.

E. The Law of Contact and Transmission was clearly involved in the case of Elisha raising the son of the Shunammite woman (II Kgs. 4:18-35).

109. WHAT PART DOES THE "LAYING ON OF HANDS" PLAY UNDER THE NEW COVENANT?

A. "Laying on of Hands" in the Name of the Lord Jesus is an appointed means by which healing for the body is ministered to the sick (Mk. 16:17-18; Lk. 4:40; 13:13).

B. "Laying on of Hands" is used to minister the Baptism in the Holy Spirit as well as to impart spiritual gifts (Acts 8:1-25; 9:1-19; 19:1-7; Rom. 1:11-12; I Cor. 1:4-8; I Tim. 4:14; II Tim. 1-6).

C. The ordination of Elders and Deacons involved the "Laying on of Hands" (Acts 6:1-6; 13:2-3).

D. The confirmation of believers involved the "Laying on of Hands" (Acts 14:21-22; 15:32).

110. WHAT IS CONFIRMATION?

Confirmation is actually viewed as a sacrament of the Church. Through the laying on of the hands of the Elders or Presbytery, members of the Church are settled, strengthened and established in the faith of Jesus Christ. Believers who have experienced or who have properly laid the following foundation stones (after being instructed in the Scriptures) may be confirmed:

A. Repentance from Dead Works

B. Faith Toward God

C. Water Baptism

D. Baptism in the Holy Spirit.
(Acts 15:32,41; 14:21-22; I Pet. 5:10)

111. HOW IS CONFIRMATION ADMINISTERED?

The most effective method of confirming the saints is through the laying on of the hands of the Elders or Presbytery of the Church (Acts. 6:6; I Tim. 4:14).

112. IS IT REALLY NECESSARY FOR US TO BE CONFIRMED?

Yes! It is necessary for us to be established in the faith so we'll not be led astray by false doctrine and deceiving spirits (Zech. 10:12; II Thes. 3:3; Rom. 1:1; 12:2).

113. WHAT IS A GOOD SUMMARY OF THE BLESSINGS OF CONFIRMATION?

A. Confirmation strengthens, settles and establishes us in the faith.

B. Confirmation gives the believer new responsibilities in the local church and causes his ministry to be acknowledged by the congregation.

C. Often times the Holy Spirit will speak through the Presbytery and commission the believer to a particular ministry or calling.

D. Whenever a commission accompanies confirmation, spiritual gifts and graces may be imparted to the believer via the laying on of the hands of the Presbytery (Ps. 68:9).

114. IS THERE MORE THAN ONE CONFIRMATION FOR BELIEVERS?

Yes! There are three kinds of confirmation which may be experienced one at a time.

A. **General Confirmation**. This is to establish the believer in the faith (I Cor. 1:5-6; II Tim. 3:14).

B. **Confirmation at the Beginning of a Ministry** (I Tim. 1:18; 4:14; II Tim. 1:6).

C. **Confirmation at the Time of Ordination** (Acts 13:1-3).

115. IS IT ALRIGHT TO LAY HANDS ON ANYONE?

No! When hands are laid upon an individual, the Law of Contact and Transmission applies. An impartation takes place. If the person receiving the ministry is an unrepentant sinner, then the one laying hands upon him becomes identified with that sinner and such identification could (but not necessarily) affect the ministry in a negative way

(I Tim. 5:22).

Conclusion

Laying on of hands is one of the foundation stones referred to in Hebrews 6:1-2. It depicts an act whereby one person lays hands upon another person, thus signifying transmission, impartation and identification. Laying on of hands is all about the law of contact and transmission. By this ministry, the people of God are blessed, healed, empowered, confirmed, ordained and sealed as able members of the New Covenant of which Jesus Christ is Lord.

Lesson Fifteen

1 Corinthians 15:20-28

20 But now is Christ risen from the dead, and become the firstfruits of them that slept.

21 For since by man came death, by man came also the resurrection of the dead.

22 For as in Adam all die, even so in Christ shall all be made alive.

23 But every man in his own order: Christ the firstfruits; afterward they that are Christ's at his coming.

24 Then cometh the end, when he shall have delivered up the kingdom to God, even the Father; when he shall have put down all rule and all authority and power.

25 For he must reign, till he hath put all enemies under his feet.

26 The last enemy that shall be destroyed is death.

27 For he hath put all things under his feet. But when he saith, all things are put under him, it is manifest that he is excepted, which did put all things under him.

28 And when all things shall be subdued unto him, then shall the Son also himself be subject unto him that put all things under him, that God may be all in all.

Resurrection of the Dead

The New Testament doctrine of the resurrection of the dead accents the fact that our Father God is the God of resurrection [Rom. 4:17]. This truth undergirds both the faith and the preaching of the Christian community and is one of the most important foundation stones that must be laid in the life of the believer.

116. WHAT ARE SOME OF THE WORDS OR TERMS USED AS A BASIS FOR OUR UNDERSTANDING OF THE TRUTH OF THE RESURRECTION?

A. Greek words:

    a. "EGEIRO," to arouse from the sleep of death.

    b. "ANISTEMI," to cause to stand up.

    c. "ANASTASIS," a raising up or a rising up.

B. English words:

    a. Awake, alive, begotten, raise, quicken, come forth.

    b. The English dictionary defines resurrection as "Revival after decay."

117. WHAT IS THE "BIBLICAL" MEANING OF RESURRECTION?

The word, resurrection, as it is used in the Bible, means "to arouse from the sleep of death," "to cause to stand up," with an emphasis upon "change." Resurrection thus involves a "rising up" of the dead (as well as a "rising up" from among the dead) with change.

118. HOW MANY RESURRECTIONS ARE THERE?

The Scriptures do not support the theory that all men will be raised at the same time in a so called "General Resurrection"; to the contrary, the Bible basically refers to two resurrections:

A. The resurrection of the Just [Jn. 5:28-29].

B. The resurrection of the Unjust [Lk. 14:14].

Note! The "resurrection of the Just" is also called the "First Resurrection," "The Resurrection of Life" and a "Better Resurrection" [cp. Heb. 11:35; Rev. 20:5].

119. WHAT DOES THE SCRIPTURES TEACH ABOUT THE "FIRST RESURRECTION?"

The Bible shows us that the "First Resurrection" consists of several stages or aspects. Observe:

A. The Resurrection of Jesus Christ

B. The Resurrection of some Old Testament saints in Jerusalem

C. The "dead in Christ" at the pre-wrath rapture

D. The Resurrection of the Old Testament saints

E. The Resurrection of "Beheaded Martyrs"

In Colossians 1:18 and Revelation 1:5, Jesus is called the "Firstborn from the dead." Here the word "Firstborn" means priority of position or rank and not priority with respect to time. Jesus is said to be "the Head of the Church," "the Beginning of the New Creation," and indeed He is all of that. This is His RANK and HIGH position. He received it by His bodily resurrection out from among the dead [cp. I Cor. 15:20ff] .

120. WHAT DOES THE RESURRECTION OF JESUS CHRIST DECLARE?

   A. Jesus is the Son of God   [Rom. 1:4]

   B. Death is defeated   [Rom. 6:9]

"We can be sure that the Risen Christ never dies again - death to touch Him is finished" (JBP).

   C. Jesus is Lord Supreme over all [cp. Mt. 28:18; Eph. 1:10]

   D. Believers are justified [Rom. 4:25].

   E. There is now a new life source for men [Acts 17:31].

   F. Future judgment is assured [Acts 17:31].

121. HOW MUST WE VIEW THE RESURRECTION OF OLD TESTAMENT SAINTS IN JERUSALEM IN MATTHEW 27:52-53?

This was a "Token Resurrection" which demonstrated the truth that Jesus Christ in His resurrection was the first fruits of them that slept. Moreover in view of the prophecy in John 12:24, it is shown that while Jesus died alone and was buried alone (in the tomb), He did not rise alone. He was then and is now the forerunner of a great harvest of "raised up ones" to come [Lev. 23:9-14].

122. WHAT ABOUT THE RESURRECTION OF THE DEAD IN CHRIST?

A. The Scriptures teach that the resurrection of the dead in Christ occurs at the Rapture. When Paul says that "the dead in Christ will rise first," he means that the dead saints are to be raised before the living saints are caught up to be with the Lord. [I THES. 4:13-16]

B. Another event that will take place, simultaneously with the resurrection of the saints is "The Rapture" or "Catching Away" of the living saints, (I Thes. 4:17]. This is Paul's way of describing the transformation of the living saints when they put on their "spiritual" bodies without passing through death.

123. WHAT ABOUT THE RESURRECTION OF THE OLD TESTAMENT SAINTS? [JOB 19:25-26; DAN. 12:1-3; ISA. 26:19-21]

Note: The following facts of Scripture seem to support a Post Tribulation view of the resurrection of Old Testament saints:

A. *Job 19:25f* places the resurrection of Old Testament saints at the time of the second coming of Christ.

B. *Daniel 12:1-3* associates the resurrection with the establishment of the Kingdom after the Great Tribulation. Cp. "My redeemer shall stand at the latter day upon the earth."

C. *Isaiah 26:19-21* associates the resurrection with the event of Christ's judgment of the world.

124. WHAT DOES THE BIBLE TEACH ABOUT THE "RESURRECTION TO DAMNATION?

The final resurrection, occurring just before the creation of the new heavens and the new earth, is that of the wicked dead. These are they who were not previously raised in any of the other resurrections. They will face final judgment at the Great White Throne, after the Millennium

[Dan. 12:2; Rev. 20:11-15].

125. IN WHAT SENSE ARE CHRISTIANS NOW RISEN?

The following scriptures explains everything:

1 AND YOU [He made alive], when you were dead (slain) by [your] trespasses and sins

5 Even when we were dead (slain) by [our own] shortcomings and trespasses, He made us alive together in fellowship and in union with Christ; [He gave us the very life of Christ Himself, the same new life with which He quickened Him, for] it is by grace (His favor and mercy which you did not deserve) that you are saved (delivered from judgment and made partakers of Christ's salvation).

6 And He raised us up together with Him and made us sit down together [giving us joint seating with Him] in the heavenly sphere [by virtue of our being] in Christ Jesus (the Messiah, the Anointed One).

Eph 2:1,5-6 AMP

19 For I through the Law [under the operation of the curse of the Law] have [in Christ's death for me] myself died to

the Law and all the Law's demands upon me, so that I may [henceforth] live to and for God.

20 I have been crucified with Christ [in Him I have shared His crucifixion]; it is no longer I who live, but Christ (the Messiah) lives in me; and the life I now live in the body I live by faith in (by adherence to and reliance on and complete trust in) the Son of God, Who loved me and gave Himself up for me.

Gal 2:19-20 AMP

14 For the love of Christ controls and urges and impels us, because we are of the opinion and conviction that [if] One died for all, then all died;

15 And He died for all, so that all those who live might live no longer to and for themselves, but to and for Him Who died and was raised again for their sake.

17 Therefore if any person is [ingrafted] in Christ (the Messiah) he is a new creation (a new creature altogether); the old [previous moral and spiritual condition] has passed away. Behold, the fresh and new has come!

2 Cor 5:14-15,17 AMP

126. HOW IS THE SPIRITUAL RESURRECTION OF THE BELIEVER SIGNIFIED?

Two Bible references tells us how our spiritual resurrection is to be set forth:

4 We were buried therefore with Him by the baptism into death, so that just as Christ was raised from the dead by the glorious [power] of the Father, so we too might [habitually] live and behave in newness of life.

5 For if we have become one with Him by sharing a death like His, we shall also be [one with Him in sharing] His resurrection [by a new life lived for God].

Rom 6:4-5 AMP

12 [Thus you were circumcised when] you were buried with Him in [your] baptism, in which you were also raised with Him [to a new life] through [your] faith in the working of God [as displayed] when He raised Him up from the dead.

Col 2:12 AMP

127. WHAT ARE SOME EVIDENCES OF THIS SPIRITUAL RESURRECTION?

A. An attitude of faith is established and maintained (Rom. 6:11)

B. A new kind of life is revealed (Rom. 6:4)

C. A new master is served and obeyed (2 Cor. 5:15)

D. A new life purpose is embraced

1 IF THEN you have been raised with Christ [to a new life, thus sharing His resurrection from the dead], aim at and seek the [rich, eternal treasures] that are above, where Christ is, seated at the right hand of God. [Ps 110:1.]

2 And set your minds and keep them set on what is above (the higher things), not on the things that are on the earth.

Col 3:1-2 AMP

Conclusion

We may summarize the Biblical truth concerning "Resurrection of the Dead" as follows:

1. The several words or terms used as a basis for understanding the truth of resurrection generally mean, "to arouse from the sleep of death," "to cause to stand up," "to raise up," and "to revive."

2. The specific Scriptural sense of resurrection always includes the necessary element of change.

3. There are basically two resurrections taught in the Bible: the resurrection of the just and the resurrection of the unjust.

4. The "First Resurrection" occurs in several stages and not all at once.

5. The Scriptural order of the First Resurrection is thus:

    a. The Resurrection of Jesus Christ.

    b. The Resurrection of "some" Old Testament saints.

    c. The Resurrection of the Dead in Christ.

    d. The Resurrection of the Old Testament saints.

    e. The Resurrection of the Tribulation saints (beheaded martyrs)

6. The "Second Resurrection" is the resurrection that is "unto damnation" and will occur after the Millennium.

7. The spiritual resurrection of the believer is called the New Birth.

Taken then as a whole, the Bible is clear that all men are destined to be raised up. "Many of them that sleep . . . shall awake, some to everlasting life and some to shame and everlasting contempt." For the righteous, the resurrection of the dead, rather than being something to fear, is actually the ground and basis of a wonderful hope.

PRAISE THE LORD!!!

Lesson Sixteen:

Revelation 20:11-15

11 And I saw a great white throne, and him that sat on it, from whose face the earth and the heaven fled away; and there was found no place for them.

12 And I saw the dead, small and great, stand before God; and the books were opened: and another book was opened, which is the book of life: and the dead were judged out of those things which were written in the books, according to their works.

13 And the sea gave up the dead which were in it; and death and hell delivered up the dead which were in them: and they were judged every man according to their works.

14 And death and hell were cast into the lake of fire. This is the second death.

15 And whosoever was not found written in the book of life was cast into the lake of fire.

ETERNAL JUDGMENT

The subject of divine judgment is one of the largest subjects in the Bible, ranging all the way from the judgment of the pre-Adamic earth, to the judgment of the cross, and ultimately to the judgment of the Great White Throne. Its great importance may be seen by reflecting for a moment on what was lost when man "fell into sin". When Adam yielded to Satan's temptation in the garden, he lost his God-given dominion and came under the awful curse of sin, sickness and death. According to Romans 8:18-25, the entire creation was affected by man's sin.

The significance of all of this to the subject of divine judgment is that redemption (if it is to be complete) must include the restoration of all that man lost in the fall; and no such redemption is possible without the full expression of the Judgment of God; for it is through judgment that every enemy of the Kingdom of God is set aside. It is through judgment that (1) righteousness prevails, (2) the curse is lifted from the earth, and (3) the saints come to share in the glory of the Lord.

128. DOES THE BIBLE PRESENT GOD AS BEING A JUDGE?

Yes! As a matter of fact, from Genesis to Revelation, God is depicted as commanding, warning, and executing judgment upon angels, men, and nations (Gen. 18:25; Jud. 11:27; Heb. 12:22-24).

129. HOW ARE WE TO UNDERSTAND THE GENERAL DEFINITION OF THE WORD JUDGMENT AS IT IS GIVEN IN THE BIBLE?

A. First of all, the word refers to the "Statutes," "Testimonies," and "Law of God." These are designed to govern and regulate covenant life. (Ps. 19; 119)

B. Secondly, the word refers to the final and also temporal estimations that God levies upon angels, men, and nations both in history and at the close of history. In this sense, "judgment" means "to separate", "to make a distinction between", "to estimate", "to bring to trial", "to call in question", "to call to account".

130. WHAT ARE SOME OF THE VARIOUS CATEGORIES OF DIVINE JUDGMENT?

A. **The Judgment of the Cross.** This is a past completed judgment wherein Jesus Christ took upon Himself the just wrath of the Father against sin (Rom.5:9-10). Four definite accomplishments may be seen in this act:

- Satan was judged and actually stripped of his authority over the Christian (Jn. 16:11; Col. 2:14-15).

- "This world" (the contra-divine system, order and arrangement headed up by Satan and characterized by force, greed, hate, competition, selfishness, and ambition) was judged and its authority broken (Jn 12:31).

- The question of sin, sickness, and disease was decisively answered in the person of Christ, our substitute (Isa. 53:4-6; Mt. 8:17; Gal. 3:13; I Pet. 2:24; II Cor. 5:21).

- Our "old man" (corrupt human nature) was judicially "destroyed," that hence forth we should not serve sin" (Rom. 6:6).

According to John 19:30, the judgment of Satan, "this world", sin, sickness and disease, along with our "old man" and "the body of sin" has been completed. "It is FINISHED" and done away with. This truth carries tremendous effect when it is allowed to become the ground of faith and confession (Mk. 11:12-24).

B. **The Judgment of the Believer in "Self-judgment" and "Chastening"**. The Scriptures teach that the believer is responsible for judging himself on a continuous basis. The meaning and content of such self-discrimination is well illustrated in the Old Testament book of Isaiah, Chapter 6;

- There is first of all the encounter with the sovereign Lord of glory, in whose light a true picture of the self is received (v. 1-4).

- Then there is the open confession of personal sin. (vs. 5; I Jn. 1:7-9)

- Next there is the application of the cleansing ministry of the Father. (vs. 6-7)

- Finally there is a restoration of divine human communication and the meaningful pursuit of a God-given task. (vs. 8-9)

- The Scriptures moreover require that, at certain specific times, self-judgment is to be carried out:

- In connection with the observance of the Lord's Supper. (I Cor. 11:28-31)
- During times of sickness. (Jas. 5:14-16)
- In the normal course of studying and feeding on the Word of God. (Ps. 119:9; Prov. 3:5-6; II Tim. 3:16f).

Note!

When the believer fails to judge or examine himself in light of the Bible, chastening results. Here, it must be observed that the normal New Testament word group pertaining to chastening or chastisement always set forth the idea of "training", "discipline", and "correction". There are other words used that tell us that the undeniable positive purpose of God is moral improvement.

The Word of God, and the Spirit of God are two different methods or means, in the New Testament by and through which divine discipline or correction is effected in the life of the believer (Jn. 14:16-17, 26; 15:26; 1:17). If and when this primary channel of training is refused, then Galatians 6:7-8 applies. In either case, whether by the Word and the Spirit, or by the enacting of the law of sowing and reaping, the Scriptures are true:

> *"Now no chastening for the present seemeth to be joyous, but grievous: nevertheless afterward it yieldeth the peaceable fruit of righteousness unto them which are exercised thereby"*
>
> Heb. 12:11

C. **The Judgment Seat of Christ.** The Scriptures clearly teach that every true believer will appear before the

"Judgment Seat of Christ" (I Pet. 4:17-18; Rom. 14:10-12; I Cor. 3:11-23; II Cor. 5:10; Col. 3:24).

Concerning this future "believers'" Judgment, the Bible teaches:

- The things which will be brought up for judgment will be "things done in the body" during life here on earth.

- It will NOT be a judgment of condemnation. (Jn. 3:18, 5:24; Rom. 8:1; Isa. 43:25; 44:22)

- Since it concerns only those who have built their faith upon the Lord Jesus, then the issue at stake is not their righteousness but the "quality" of their service rendered to Christ. In other words, the real purpose of the judgment here it to determine the reward due to each believer, as well as his or her place in the coming Millennial Reign of Christ.

- Many believers will receive crowns:

    1) The Crown of Life (Jas. 1:12; Rev. 2:10)

    2) The Crown of Glory (I Pet. 5:1-4)

    3) The Crown of Righteousness (II Tim. 4:7-8)

    4) The Crown of Rejoicing (I Thes. 2:19-20)

    5) The Incorruptible Crown for Self-Mastery. (I Cor. 9:24-25)

D. **The Judgment of the Gentile Nations.**

On the first day of the Millennium, after Satan is bound and thrown into the abyss (Rev. 20:1-3), a tremendous judgment will fall upon the Gentile nations who survive the ordeals of the "The Day of the Lord." The Sheep nations (those Gentiles who befriend Israel during the day of the Lord) will be pronounced "blessed of my Father" and will hence enter the Kingdom. The goat nations (those Gentiles who took sides with the beast and the false prophet) will be pronounced "cursed" and will depart and be held for destruction in everlasting fire, prepared for the devil and his angels (Mt. 25:31-46).

Note! The brethren referred to in Matthew 25:40 are "whosoever doeth the will of the Father" (Mt. 12:49-50).

E. **The Judgment of the Great White Throne.** Concerning this final judgment (Rev. 20:1115), the Scriptures teach the following:

- This judgment refers only to the wicked.
- The Lord Jesus Christ Himself is the Judge (Jn. 5:27).
- Satan and fallen angels will be judged and condemned once for all.
- Judgment will proceed on the basis of the record contained in "the books":

1) The Book of Life (Rev. 20:12, 15)
2) The Bible (Jn. 12:48)
3) The Book of Memory (Lk. 16:25)
4) The Book of Conscience (Rom. 2:15-16)
5) The Book of Character (Lk 12:22; Jer. 17:1)
6) The Book of Nature

Conclusion

All in all, the subject of eternal judgment is one of the most important subjects in the Bible. It is God's chosen way of removing all enemy obstructions to the full establishment of His Kingdom. This is how righteousness prevails, the curse is lifted, and the saints come to share in the glory of the Lord.

The Redeemed Community

Section Four

GOALS AND OBJECTIVES

- To understand the nature, structure and destiny of the church.
- To understand the ministry and gifts of the Holy Spirit.
- To understand church membership and commitment.
- To understand the biblical truth re: marriage, divorce and remarriage.

A COVENANT COMMUNITY

A community of God's redeemed people bound together in covenant love, submitted to compassionate authority and rulership and manifesting peace, holiness and family fidelity expressed through revered fatherhood, cherished woman and motherhood with secure and obedient children.

A community where loving correction and instruction produce healthy growth and maturity, where dedication to excellence produces the finest result in arts, crafts, trades and commerce, providing prosperity and abundance for all its members.

A community where all life is inspired and directed by the Spirit of Jesus Christ and is lived to His glory as a witness and testimony to the world.

by Don Basham

Lesson Seventeen:

Isaiah 2:2

2 And it shall come to pass in the last days, that the mountain of the Lord's house shall be established in the top of the mountains, and shall be exalted above the hills; and all nations shall flow unto it.

Matthew 16:13-19

13 When Jesus came into the coasts of Caesarea Philippi, he asked his disciples, saying, Whom do men say that I the Son of man am?

14 And they said, Some say that thou art John the Baptist: some, Elias; and others, Jeremias, or one of the prophets.

15 He saith unto them, But whom say ye that I am?

16 And Simon Peter answered and said, Thou art the Christ, the Son of the living God.

17 And Jesus answered and said unto him, Blessed art thou, Simon Barjona: for flesh and blood hath not revealed it unto thee, but my Father which is in heaven.

18 And I say also unto thee, That thou art Peter, and upon this rock I will build my church; and the gates of hell shall not prevail against it.

19 And I will give unto thee the keys of the kingdom of heaven: and whatsoever thou shalt bind on earth shall be bound in heaven: and whatsoever thou shalt loose on earth shall be loosed in heaven.

THE NEW COVENANT CHURCH

Through the restored ministry gifts of apostles, prophets, evangelists, pastors and teachers, our Lord Jesus Christ is building His church. The Scriptures teach that this is a top priority in the end-time purpose of God.

131. WHAT HAS THE WORD OF GOD REVEALED CONCERNING THE CHURCH?

The Scriptures reveal that God has His own people, His own congregation, i.e., His own Church right here in the midst of this corrupt world system. This church is "in the world but not of the world" and we know this Church by faith in the Word of God. (Mat. 16:18-19; 21:42-43; Phil. 3:1-3; I Pet 2:9-10).

Note!

By testing "congregations of people" by the Word of God, we'll be able to identify the true Church of Jesus Christ, and distinguish it from the false church i.e., the bride of the Anti-Christ.

132. WHAT IS THE "CATHOLIC" OR "UNIVERSAL" CHRISTIAN CHURCH REFERRED TO IN THE APOSTLE'S CREED?

The "catholic" or "universal" Christian Church referred to in the creed is the corporate body of all born again believers in the Lord Jesus Christ, gathered out of the world from Pentecost up to the First Resurrection. It is the spiritual kingdom of

Christ, and it extends beyond all denominational boundaries (Heb. 12:22-23; Rev. 21:9-10; Ps. 48:1-2).

133. DID GOD HAVE A PEOPLE OR A CHURCH UNDER THE OLD COVENANT?

Yes! God actually began gathering "His people" together right after the Fall of Man (Gen. 3:15). This gathering together of "His own" continues unto this day. Observe the activity of God:

- A. **From Adam to Abraham**, Christ gathered "His people" from the descendants of Adam. (Gen. 4:26)

- B. **From Abraham to Christ**, "the people of God" are gathered from the family of Abraham, through Isaac and Jacob. (Gen. 12:1-3; 15:5-6; 28:3-4)

- C. **From Pentecost to the return of Christ**, "the Church of Jesus Christ" is being gathered from the nations of the world.

Note!

Through disobedience, Israel violated God's covenant, and God then promised to institute a New Covenant and a New Covenant people consisting of both Jews and Gentiles (Isa. 1:2-4; Jer. 2; 31:31-34).

> *Know ye therefore that they which are of faith, the same are the children of Abraham, So then they which be of faith are blessed with faithful Abraham. Christ hath redeemed us from the curse of the law, being made a curse for us: for it is written, Cursed is every one that hangeth on a tree: That the blessing of Abraham might come on the Gentiles through Jesus Christ: that we might receive the promise of the Spirit*

through faith. For ye are all the children of God by faith in Christ Jesus. And if ye be Christ's then are ye Abraham's seed, and heirs according to the promise. (Galatians 3:7, 9, 13, 14, 26, 29)

134. WHAT MYSTERIES HAVE BEEN REVEALED TO US CONCERNING THE UNION OF THE LORD JESUS CHRIST AND HIS CHURCH?

Actually, several mysteries or "hidden truths" are set forth in the Scriptures concerning the Church and the Lord Jesus Christ.

   A. The Church is a fatherhood in history that is also (at the same time) a fatherhood beyond history.

For this cause I bow my knees unto the Father of our Lord Jesus Christ, Of whom the whole family in heaven and earth is named.

Ephesians 3:14-15

Note!

The Lord Jesus Christ has established in the earth a family that's headed up by a father (the Greek word for family in Eph. 3:15 means fatherhood). This family is at one and the same time a visible society and a spiritual community (Acts 2:40-47).

   B. The Church is The Body of Christ and the Lord Jesus Christ is the Head of that body (Eph. 4:25; 5:30).

And he is the head of the body, the church: which is the beginning the firstborn from the dead: that in all things he might have the preeminence. Colossians 1:18

C. The Church is the Bride of Christ and the object of His divine love.

Husbands, love your wives, even as Christ also loved the church, and gave himself for it;

That he might sanctify and cleanse it with the washing of water by the word.

That he might present it to himself a glorious church, not having spot, or wrinkle, or any such thing; but that it should be holy and without blemish.

So ought men to love their wives as their own bodies. He that loveth his wife loveth himself.

For no man ever yet hated his own flesh; but nourisheth and cherisheth it, even as the Lord the church:

For we are members of his body, of his flesh, and of his bones.

For this cause shall a man leave his father and mother and shall be joined unto his wife, and they two shall be one flesh.

This is a great mystery: but I speak concerning Christ and the church.

Ephesians 5:25-32

D. The Church is a branch in Christ — The Vine.

I am the vine, ye are the branches; He that abideth in me, and I in him, the same bringeth forth much fruit; for without me ye can do nothing.

John 15:5

E. The Church is the temple of the Holy Spirit. (II Cor. 6:16; Eph. 2:21-22; Rev. 21:3)

Know ye not that ye are the temple of God, and that the Spirit of God dwelleth in you?

If any man defile the temple of God, him shall God destroy; for the temple of God is holy, which temple ye are.

I Corinthians 3:16-17

F. Outside of the Church i.e., outside of the Redeemed Community of which the Lord Jesus Christ is head, there is no salvation. All salvation comes from the Lord Jesus Christ, through His Church. When He calls us to salvation, He actually brings us into "His Flock" and into "His Fold". Thus, we are totally joined to Him.

(Jn. 10:16; I Cor. 6:17)

For by one Spirit are we all baptized into one body, whether we be Jews or Gentiles, whether we be bond or free; and have been all made to drink into one Spirit.

I Corinthians 12:13

135. WHAT IS THE LOCAL CHURCH?

A. By definition, the "local church" is that part of the "universal church" that is resident in a given locality.

B. The broad requirements for membership in such a local body are:

1. A correct relationship to the Lord Jesus Christ.

2. Residence in a geographical locality.

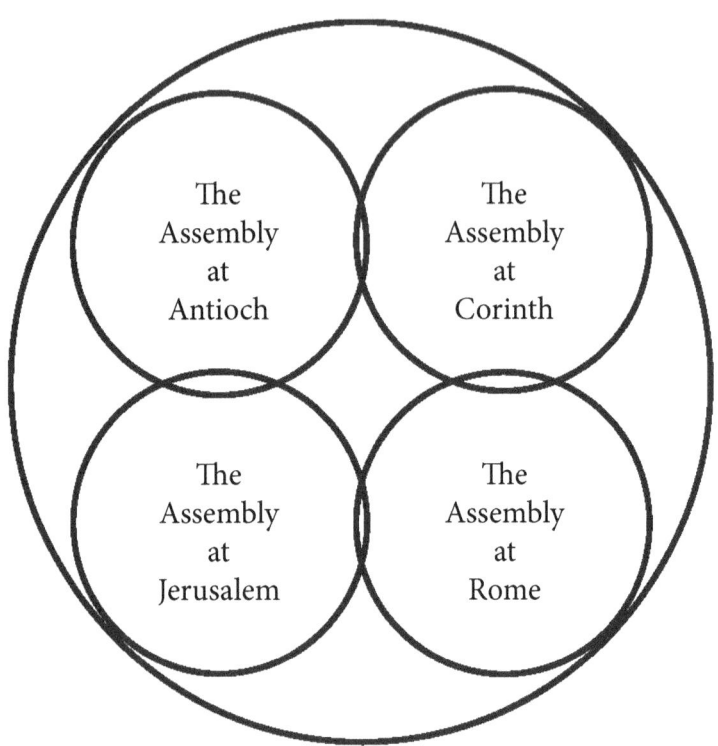

Note!

Within each of these local churches (which are identified geographically) there are many "cell" churches of various sizes and cultural distinctions, etc. The differences between these "cells" does not (or should not) overshadow the essential unity that exists throughout the true churches of Christ in the area. In this study, references to "the local church" are more truly references to the many "cell" churches within a given geographical setting i.e., within the church at Detroit.

136. HOW DOES A LOCAL CHURCH PROPERLY EMERGE?

A. The first phase of the development of a local church involves the gathering together of an initial "cell" of two or three believers "in the name of the Lord Jesus Christ."

Verily I say unto you, Whatsoever ye shall bind on earth shall be bound in heaven and whatsoever ye shall loose on earth shall be loosed in heaven.

Again I say unto you, That if two of you shall agree on earth as touching any thing that they shall ask, it shall be done for them of my Father which is in heaven.

For where two or three are gathered together in my name, there am I in the midst of them.

Matthew 18:18-20

Note!

The Holy Spirit does not gather believers around human personalities, ordinances, or denominations.

B. The second phase of local church development is seen in the Scriptures. Through the preaching of the gospel, believers are obtained and then discipled or taught. These "discipled believers" are later confirmed and strengthened in the faith. Also, at this second phase, spiritually mature men (elders) are ordained to serve as a leadership team in the local assembly.

And when they had preached the gospel to that city, and had taught many, they returned again to Lystra and to Iconium, and Antioch,

Confirming the souls of the disciples, and exhorting them to continue in the faith, and that we must through much tribulation enter into the kingdom of God.

And when they had ordained them elders in every church and had prayed with fasting, they commended them to the Lord on whom they believed.

Acts 14:21-23

C. At phase three of the development of the local church, the leadership ministries are completed and the church looks like the following:

Paul and Timotheus, the servants of Jesus Christ, to all the saints in Christ Jesus which are at Philippi, with the bishops and deacons:

Philippians 1:1

Observe again the text in Philippians and see that a properly established church will have local and translocal (apostolic and prophetic) ministry.

D. In the final or fourth phase of the development of a local church, non-leadership, congregational ministries will emerge.

For to one is given by the Spirit the word of wisdom: to another the word of knowledge by the same Spirit; To another faith by the same Spirit; to another the gifts of healing by the same Spirit;

To another the working of miracles; to another prophecy; to another discerning of spirits; to another divers kinds of tongues; to another the interpretation of tongues.

1 Corinthians 12:8-10

137. WHAT DOES IT MEAN TO SAY THAT THE LORD JESUS CHRIST IS THE HEAD OF THE CHURCH?

A. It means that the Lord Jesus Christ is the Absolute, Sovereign Administrator of all things.
(Eph. 1:22; Col. 1:18)

B. It means that the Lord Jesus Christ alone exercises Rulership, Imperial Authority and Government with respect to the Redeemed Community.
(Isa. 9:6-9; 22:20-24; Eph. 4:15; 5:23-27; Col. 2:10)

C. It means that the Lord Jesus Christ, through the several "means of grace" set in the church, nourishes, cleanses, purifies, feeds, and cares for the members of His spiritual body.

Note!

Broadly speaking, "means of grace" is a term that refers to whatever may minister to the spiritual welfare of believers, such as the following:

- The Preaching of the Word
- The Sacraments of the church
- Prayer

138. WHAT DOES ISAIAH 32:1-4 AND JOHN 10 TEACH US REGARDING HOW THE LORD JESUS CHRIST GOVERNS HIS CHURCH?

The Lord Jesus Christ rules or governs His church through delegated authorities. Note the following biblical pattern:

A. God the Father was represented by God the Son, who in turn was represented by His disciples.
(Mt. 10:40; Lk. 10:16)

B. To receive the representatives of Christ is equivalent to receiving Christ Himself. As a matter of fact, our inner attitude toward those who are over us in the Lord expresses how we really feel about our Lord, Jesus Christ.

139. WHAT ARE THE DELEGATED AUTHORITIES SET IN THE BODY OF CHRIST?

Wherefore he saith, When he ascended up on high, he led captivity captive, and gave gifts unto men.

(Now that he ascended, what is it but that he also descended first into the lower parts of the earth?

He that descended is the same also that ascended up far above all heavens, that he might fill all things.)

And he gave some, apostles; and some, prophets; and some, evangelists; and some, pastors and teachers.

Ephesians 4:8-11

A. These are the gifts Christ has given to the Church:

Apostle: One sent as a messenger, the bearer of a commission, church planter, spiritual father of churches.
(Eph. 4:11; I Cor. 12:28)

Prophet: A Spokesman for another, an interpreter for God, a seer, a divinely commissioned and inspired person, a foreteller of the future, one gifted for the exposition of the truth.
(Acts 15)

Evangelist: One who announces glad tidings, one who enlarges and extends the kingdom of God, one who shares in edifying and building the Church.
(Eph. 4:11; Acts 21:8; II Tim. 4:5)

Pastor: One who tends the sheep, a shepherd, one who cares for the sheep, one who leads, feeds, waters and guards the sheep, a guardian.
(Jn. 10:16; 21:16; I Pet. 5:2-3)

Teacher: One who instructs, the occupation of teaching, someone qualified to instruct others, someone who imparts Bible truth to others.
(I Tim. 3:2; II Tim. 2:2, 4; I Cor. 12:28; Rom. 12:6)

B. These "gifts" are properly called "equipping" gifts because they train committed believers for the work of the ministry.
(Eph 4:12-16)

C. The local Presbytery of Elders:

1. The titles of Elder, Bishop and Shepherd are often used interchangeably.
(Acts 20:17, 28; Tit. 1:5-7; I Pet. 5:1-5)

- Elder: A spiritually mature man or male.

- Bishop: The office or position of overseer or superintendent.

- Shepherd: The job or work performed to feed; to lead; to care for; to protect; to rule.

2. The Scriptures support the idea of a plurality of elders ministering together at the local level.

(Acts 14:23; 15:2, 4, 6, 22-23; Jas. 5:14)

Note!

All elders in the local church do not have the same or equal authority and honor. One elder is always recognized as having been raised up and anointed by the Holy Spirit to be "Leader of the group", "First among equals", "Chief Elder", "Senior Pastor", "Set Man", etc. He will be the spokesman and representative of the presbytery and leadership team in the church.

(Acts 2:14; 15:12-20; 21:18-25; Rev. 1:4, 11; 2:1—the church is addressed via the angel—Chief Elder/Senior Pastor of the church.)

140. WHAT ARE SOME BIBLICAL QUALIFICATIONS FOR ELDERS, SHEPHERDS OR OVERSEERS?

A. Submissive attitude.
   (I Pet. 5:5; Eph. 5:21)

B. Faithfulness
   (Lk. 16:10-12; II Tim. 2:1-2)

C. The Scriptures give us many more qualifications for these positions in I Timothy 3:1-7 and Titus 1:5-9.

141. IS IT PROPER THAT THE SAINTS IN THE LOCAL CHURCH SERVE AND HONOR THE SHEPHERDS WHO ARE OVER THEM IN THE LORD?

The answer is clearly, yes! [cp. Isa. 52:7; Rom. 2:10, 13:7; I Cor. 9:11-14; Gal. 6:6; I Tim. 5:17-18, 6:1].

Observe that the scriptures portray a servant as one who gives himself up to the will and purpose of another [cp. Lk. 17:7-10 and Dt. 15-12-18]. Such a person shows a deep love for God by thus serving others.... [cp. Gal. 5:13-14 and I Jn. 3:16]. Needless to say, the Lord bountifully rewards such faithfulness [cp. II Kg. 3:11; Mt. 25:14-30; Col. 3:22-25].

142. WHAT IS HONOR?

By definition, "honor" is manifested respect or esteem. It is both an attitude and an act of recognition.

143. WHERE DOES HONOR COME FROM?

According to the scriptures, even though the saints or believers are involved, God is actually the source of honor [cp. I Kings 3:13; I Chron. 29:10-13; II Chron. 1:9-12; I Sam. 2:30].

144. WHAT ARE SOME BIBLICAL REASONS FOR BESTOWING HONOR UPON SHEPHERDS?

A. Because he is a man of humility and reverences and fears the Lord [cp. Prov. 22:4; I Pet. 5:6].

B. Because he is a man of uprightness and right standing with God [cp. Prov. 14:34].

C. Because of his godly wisdom; i.e., comprehensive insight into the ways and purposes of God [cp. Prov. 12:8].

D. Because he's not too big to receive corrections [cp. Prov. 12:1-2, 15:31].

E. Because he earnestly seeks after mercy and lovingkindness [cp. Prov. 21:21].

145. HOW IS HONOR TO BE SHOWN OR DEMONSTRATED?

Earlier we observed that honor was both an attitude and an act.

Without a demonstration, proper and noble attitudes will remain incomplete and thus void of power.

Study the Old Testament book of Esther 6:1-11 and note carefully the honor bestowed upon Mordecai.

- He was publicly acclaimed.

- He was given a promotion in authority.

- Gifts (including clothing) were given.

- He was given royal or kingly service and respect; i.e., the red carpet treatment.

The willingness and the ability of the saints to serve and honor their spiritual overseers "as unto the Lord" is a direct clue to the kind of fellowship they have with the Lord Jesus Christ. One who is in good fellowship with the Lord will have no problem honoring those whom the Savior honors.

Conclusion

It is the will of God that true believers live their lives in covenant with Jesus Christ and His saints, in a community (church)

where the Holy Spirit is free to move among the people. This community of the redeemed, when it is built right, will express righteousness, peace and joy in the Holy Spirit, all to the glory of God.

Lesson Eighteen:

Acts 2:40-42

40 And with many other words did he testify and exhort, saying, Save yourselves from this untoward generation.

41 Then they that gladly received his word were baptized: and the same day there were added unto them about three thousand souls.

42 And they continued stedfastly in the apostles' doctrine and fellowship, and in breaking of bread, and in prayers.

The Meeting and Mission of the Church

If we are to understand what the New Testament teaches about the doctrine and practice of the Church, then, it's important that we distinguish two kinds of meetings. The first is "The Church Meeting. The second is similar to what we call "church services" today. In this latter meeting, usually one man is featured. He stands before the congregation, and, by his teaching or preaching, directs the thoughts and hearts of the saints. The Apostle Paul regularly held meetings like this in Corinth and Ephesus. (Acts 18:7-8; 19:8-10)

In this lesson, however, we'll focus our attention upon the other kind of meeting — the kind that New Covenant believers enjoyed, and which is described in considerable detail in Scripture. Concerning this meeting, one Bible teacher says,

"I cannot imagine anything that could be more dynamic, or exciting, more meaningful, relevant, or edifying for me as a Christian, and more glorifying to the Lord, than a church meeting — New Testament style."

146. WHAT IS "THE CHURCH MEETING"?

A. It is first of all a diverse meeting.

The earliest New Testament churches didn't just meet to hear a sermon, or to celebrate the Lord's supper. To the contrary, the church meeting had various elements.

> *And they continued steadfastly in the apostles' doctrine and fellowship, and in breaking of bread, and in prayers.*
>
> Acts 2:42

Note!

<u>Teaching</u>, <u>prayer</u>, <u>fellowship</u>, and <u>the breaking of bread</u>, were always a part of the gathering of the believers in Jerusalem.

This same pattern is seen at Corinth.

> *How is it then, brethren? when ye come together, every one of you hath a psalm, hath a doctrine, hath a tongue, hath a revelation, hath an interpretation. Let all things be done unto edifying.*
>
> I Corinthians 14:26

Observe here that the church meeting involved several elements: music, doctrine, the operation of spiritual giftings, and revelation. And, what is also important to this meeting is the fact that all of the saints participated. The meeting in other words, was diverse in content and participation.

B. It is, secondly, a Christ-centered meeting.

This feature of New Covenant church life is clearly indicated in Acts 20:7. Here, the saints meet together to "remember the Lord Jesus Christ", to hear from Him and to celebrate His Name, and it all centers around the breaking of bread.

Properly observing the Lord's Supper here has the effect of focusing the attention of the Saints on the Lord Jesus Christ — His glorious person, and His mighty works.

The Apostle Paul moreover explains why this Christ-centered focus must be made:

And he is before all things and by him all things consist.

And he is the head of the body, the church: who is the beginning, the firstborn from the dead; that in all things he might have the preeminence.

For it pleased the Father that in him should all fulness dwell.

Colossians 1:17-19

Let the word of Christ dwell in you richly in all wisdom; teaching and admonishing one another in psalms and hymns and spiritual songs, singing with grace in your hearts to the Lord

And whatsoever ye do in word or deed, do all in the name of the Lord Jesus, giving thanks to God and the Father by him.

Colossians 3:16-17

Obviously, He who is the Head of the Church, and the Lord of all is the only one who should have the preeminence.

> C. The church meeting is, thirdly, a meeting that is open, free and spontaneous…a meeting where joys can be shared and burdens can be borne. Stated differently, it is a meeting that's completely available to the person and ministry of the Holy Spirit. The words of the Apostle regarding such a meeting are quite appropriate: "Quench not the Spirit".
> (I Thess. 5:19-21)

The lesson here is that the Holy Spirit of God has been sent into the Church and actually indwells it as the representative of Christ. In the meeting of the Church, the Holy Spirit guides and oversees everything. This means that, there will be no confusion; for, God is not the author of confusion. The Holy Spirit will always bring about order.   (I Cor. 14:26-40)

For the record, extreme formality, tradition, clock-watching and a critical spirit can effectively quench the free, spontaneous flow of the Spirit of God in any meeting of the church.

147. WHAT IS THE TWO-FOLD PURPOSE OF THE CHURCH MEETING?

A. First of all, the church meeting is for the edification or building up of believers. This can be achieved through music ministry, the ministry of the Word, or through personal testimonies.
(I Cor. 14:26; Acts 14:27; 15:4, 12)

B. Secondly, the church meeting is for the worship or adoration of the Lord. According to the Scriptures, New Covenant worship must be "in spirit" and "in truth". To say that it must be "in spirit" is to say that, true worship is a person-to-Person experience, honoring the God and Father of our Lord, Jesus Christ. This experience takes place in and through our reborn human spirit and not in our "flesh". To say that true worship must be "in truth" simply means that it must be genuine and without pretense. In other words, it must be in harmony with the truth or Word of God.
(Jn. 4:24; Mt. 15:8-9)

148. WHAT DO THE SCRIPTURES TEACH CONCERNING THE MISSION OF THE CHURCH?

And he said unto them, It is not for you to know the times or the seasons, which the Father hath put in his own power.

> *But ye shall receive power, after that the Holy Ghost is come upon you: and ye shall be witnesses unto me both in Jerusalem, and in all Judea, and in Samaria and unto the uttermost part of the earth.*
>
> Acts 1:7-8

A. The first and primary objective of the Church is to be a (corporate) witness unto the Lord Jesus Christ. The emphasis here is upon being something i.e., existing in the world in a certain "God ordained manner".

(I Thess. 1:2-8)

> *And so you became a model to all the believers in Macedonia and Achaia.*
>
> *The Lord's message rang out from you not only in Macedonia and Achaia—your faith in God has become known everywhere. Therefore we do not need to say anything about it.*
>
> I Thessalonians 1:7-8 NIV

Observe! The Church, first of all, became a model. Then, after they had become something, God caused them to effectively do something.

"The Lord's Message rang out..."

The Divine Pattern is clear: Being precedes doing! The model precedes the message! Note Paul's words to young Timothy:

Let no man despise thy youth; but be thou an example of the believers, in word, in conversation, in charity, in spirit, in faith, in purity.

I Timothy 4:12

B. The Church has been called to be the guardian and support of the Truth.

These things write I unto thee, hoping to come unto thee shortly:

But if I tarry long, that thou mayest know how thou oughtest to behave thyself in the house of God, which is the church of the living God, the pillar and ground of the truth.

I Timothy 3:14-15

The truth referred to here is the kind of truth that's found in the Lord Jesus Christ and the Word of God. It must be guarded and published by the Church. Any congregation of Christians who'll not do this will tragically become the pillar and ground of error instead of truth.

C. The Church is the Authorized, Visible, Representative of Christ. This means that Jesus Christ is now carrying on a two-fold work in the world through the Church.

As thou hast sent me into the world, even so have I also sent them into the world.

John 17:18

Then said Jesus to them again, Peace be unto you: as my Father hath sent me, even so send I you.

John 20:21

1. Jesus ministers to the physical and material needs of men through the Church.

(Mt. 25:31-45; Lk. 4:18-19)

But whoso hath this world's good, and seeth his brother have need, and shutteth up his bowls of compassion from him, how dwelleth the love of God in him?

I John 3:17

If a brother or sister be naked, and destitute of daily food,

And one of you say unto them, Depart in peace, be warmed and filled; notwithstanding ye give them not those things which are needful to the body; what doth it profit?

Even so faith, if it hath not works, is dead being alone.

James 2:15-17

2. Jesus ministers to the spiritual needs of men through the Church.

For the Son of man came to seek and to save that which was lost.

Luke 19:10

For God sent not his son into the world to condemn the world; but that the world through him might be saved.

John 3:15

This is a faithful saying, and worthy of all acceptation, that Christ Jesus came into the world to save sinners; of whom I am chief.

I Timothy 1:15

Note!

In light of these Scriptures, it's not proper for the Church to turn it's God-given mission over to governmental agencies or social welfare systems.

149. WHERE IS THE FIELD OF LABOR FOR THE CHURCH? WHAT (IN OTHER WORDS) IS THE SCOPE OF THE WORK OF THE CHURCH?

A. The Church is to minister to the needs of its members. (Eph. 4:11-15; Col. 1:28)

Pure religion and undefiled before God and the Father is this, To visit the fatherless and widows in their affliction, and to keep himself unspotted from the world.

James 1:27

Is any sick among you? let him call for the elders of the church; and let them pray over him, anointing him with oil in the name of the Lord.

James 5:14

B. The Church is to exercise a wholesome discipline over its members.

Brethren, if a man be overtaken in a fault, ye which are spiritual, restore such an one in the spirit of meekness; considering thyself, lest thou also be tempted.

Galatians 6:1

1. Private Offenses must be dealt with. These are differences or conflicts between individual members that Jesus said should be handled according to Matthew 18:15-17. Observe how Paul upbraided the saints at Corinth for going to the heathen courts in order to sue each other.

But brother goeth to law with brother, and that before the unbelievers.

Now therefore there is utterly a fault among you, because ye go to law one with another. Why do ye not rather take wrong? why do ye not rather suffer yourselves to be defrauded?

I Corinthians 6:6-7

2. Public Offenses must be dealt with. These are moral or doctrinal lapses that "go public" i.e., "make the news".

In the spirit of love, the church leadership should attempt to reclaim and restore those who have thus fallen. If they persist in their evil ways, the Scriptures are clear.

(II Thes. 3:6)

To deliver such an one unto Satan for the destruction of the flesh, that the spirit man may be saved in the day of the Lord Jesus.

But them that are without God judgeth. Therefore put away from among yourselves that wicked person.

I Corinthians 5:5, 13

It must be noted here that a sinning brother or sister should be restored to the church fellowship when they show signs of repentance.

(II Cor. 2:6-7)

C. The Church has a duty to the world community. (Mt. 13:38; 28:19; Acts 1:8)

This will involve, among other things, seeking to bring all within its reach to a saving knowledge of the Lord Jesus Christ. In this connection, there are three great truths that the Church cannot escape:

1. The whole world needs the Gospel.

We know that we are children of God, and that the whole world is under the control of the evil one.

I John 5:19 (NIV)

2. The Gospel is sufficient for the whole world.

And he is the propitiation for our sins: and not for ours only, but also for the sins of the whole world.

I John 2:2

To be sure, there will never be a need for another savior. What Jesus did in His death on the cross is still sufficient for all the world.

3. The Lord Jesus Christ has commissioned His Church to give the Gospel to the whole world.

And he said unto them, Go ye into all the world, and preach the gospel to every creature.

Mark 16:15

150. How did the earliest New Testament churches carry on their mission? What was their method?

    A. Jesus called the Church to a public ministry of preaching i.e., a ministry of proclaiming the Lordship of Jesus Christ and the sufficiency of His death, burial, resurrection and exaltation.
(I Cor. 1:21)

    B. Personal Work

Having then gifts differing according to the grace that is given to us, whether prophecy, let us prophesy according to the proportion of faith;

Or ministry, let us wait on our ministering: or he that teacheth, on teaching;

Or he that exhorteth, on exhortation: he that giveth, let him do it with simplicity; he that ruleth, with diligence; he that sheweth mercy, with cheerfulness.

Romans 12:6-8

Every member of the Church has his own place to fill. This is called "Body Ministry" and involves the following:

    1. Personal witness

If a true believer has the passion of Christ in his heart he will find a way to witness for the Lord. (Acts 8:4)

2. Prayer

(Phil. 4:6; I Thes. 5:17)

3. Giving

(I Cor. 16:1-3; Phil 4:15-18)

C. Cooperation or teamwork

By definition, a team is two or more people, who are interacting (communicating) and aiming at the same goal. Not only must individual Christians work together, but local churches must also work together.

> *If there be therefore any consolation in Christ, if any comfort of love, if any fellowship of the Spirit, if any bowels and mercies,*
>
> *Fulfil ye my joy, that ye be like-minded, having the same love, being of one accord, of one mind.*
>
> *Let nothing be done through strife or vainglory, but in lowliness of mind let each esteem other better than themselves.*
>
> *Look not every man on his own things, but every man also on the things of others.*
>
> Philippians 2:1-4
>
> *But now I go unto Jerusalem to minister unto the saints.*

For it hath pleased them of Macedonia and Achaia to make a certain contribution for the poor saints which are at Jerusalem.

Romans 15:25-26

These funds were treated as a sacred trust and was to be used to underwrite the mission of the Church of Jesus Christ. They were given for a definite purpose, and Paul and his associates had no authority to divert them to other causes, even if they wanted to.

(II Cor. 16-21 NRSV)

151. WHAT IS BODY MINISTRY?

The term, "body ministry" means ministry by the Body. It's every member of the local congregation of Spirit-filled believers exercising or performing the "gifted ministry" that God set them in the Body to fulfill. The Apostle Paul lists these ministries in I Corinthians 12:27-28; Romans 12:6-8; and Ephesians 4:11-13.

"Now you are together the Body of Christ, and each of you is a part of it. And in the Church God has appointed first, some to be His messengers, secondly, some to be preachers, of power, thirdly teachers. After them He has appointed workers of spiritual power, men with the gift of healing, helpers, counsellors and those with the gift of speaking various tongues."

I Corinthians 12:27-28
(J.B. Phillips Modern English)

These references support the teaching that God has chosen (in this dispensation) to use the whole body of believers, functioning "charismatically" to accomplish His purpose in the world. This is clearly the meaning of the commission that Jesus gave to the Church:

> *"And these signs will follow those who believe: In My name they will cast out demons; they will speak with new tongues;*
>
> *They will take up serpents; and if they drink anything deadly, it will by no means hurt them; they will lay hands on the sick, and they will recover"*
>
> Mark 16:17-18 NKJV

Note the Text! The promise of our Lord is that He would confirm the Word "with signs following", not just for Apostles, but for "those who believe". He's talking about body ministry.

(I Cor. 11; Joel 2:28)

Thus we see that it is no longer just the anointed prophet who receives revelations and speaks by the Spirit; to the contrary, the many-membered, Spirit-filled, Body of Christ receives revelation and speaks out exhorting, edifying, comforting and ministering in the power and demonstration of the Holy Spirit.

All of this suggests that the restoration of the ascension-gift ministries of Apostles, Prophets, Evangelists, Shepherds and Teachers is a must.

> *And he gave some, apostles; and some, prophets; and some, evangelists; and some, pastors and teachers;*
>
> *For the perfecting of the saints, for the work of the ministry, for the edifying of the body of Christ:*
>
> Ephesians 4:11-12

Observe! Here it is stated that the Lord Jesus Christ gave "gifted men" to the Church for the edifying, equipping and preparing of the saints for the work of the ministry. This is both clear and concise. However, it became complicated and confused when the Professing Denominational Church rejected the Baptism into the Holy Spirit, along with its consequent pentecostal giftings. When this occurred man's order replaced God's Due Order. The Ascension-gift ministries disappeared. Apostles were replaced by missionary boards and societies; Prophets, who could "see", were replaced by preachers who did research and delivered nice little Bible stories; evangelistic associations (trained in Madison Avenue promotional techniques) replaced anointed men like Philip (Acts 8); men with genuine Teaching ministries (like Apollos) were exchanged for Sunday School teachers, and directors of religious education who only majored in the "letter of the Word"; and real Pastors and Elders were replaced with business administrators and corporate executives who demonstrated little to nothing of a shepherd's heart. With leaders like this, it's no wonder the local church is in the mess that it's in.

But thank God, we are beginning to see a change. In spite of strong opposition, real Apostolic and Prophetic ministry is being raised up in the Church; wise master builders are now laying the foundation stones that will undergird a new habitation of God in the Spirit. Saints are finally being equipped and perfected so that they can get out and do the work of the ministry.

DO YOU HAVE A DEFINITE FUNCTION IN THE BODY?

Conclusion

All in all, then, this is the way we may summarize God's purpose, as far as the meeting and the mission of the Church is concerned. It's all about evangelism and nurturing, saving the lost and edifying the Saints.

Jesus said in Matthew 16:18, "I will build my church; and the gates of hell shall not prevail against it". Then, just prior to leaving them to carry on His work and to fulfill His prophetic words, Jesus said, "Go, and as you go, make disciples (win men to Christ); baptize them, build them up so that they'll walk in the same instruction, revelation and truth that I've given to you..." This assignment of evangelism and nurturing is what the meeting and the mission of the Church is all about.

Lesson Nineteen

Acts 2:41-47

41 Then they that gladly received his word were baptized: and the same day there were added unto them about three thousand souls.

42 And they continued stedfastly in the apostles' doctrine and fellowship, and in breaking of bread, and in prayers.

43 And fear came upon every soul: and many wonders and signs were done by the apostles.

44 And all that believed were together, and had all things common;

45 And sold their possessions and goods, and parted them to all men, as every man had need.

46 And they, continuing daily with one accord in the temple, and breaking bread from house to house, did eat their meat with gladness and singleness of heart,

47 Praising God, and having favour with all the people. And the Lord added to the church daily such as should be saved.

The Sacraments of the Church

In order to understand the Sacraments of the Church, we must first understand the term, "means of grace". This term, in the broad general sense, refers to whatever may, from time to time, minister to the spiritual welfare of believers. More specifically, the term refers to the Word of God and the Sacraments. These are the channels through which the Grace of God comes to the believer in the Redeemed Community. The Word is intended to birth and strengthen faith. The Sacraments can only strengthen it. On the other hand, God's Word goes out into all the world, while the Sacraments are administered only to those believers who are able members of the New Covenant.

(Jn. 1:1 ff.; Ps. 33:6; Heb. 1:3; II Tim. 3:15 ff.)

152. WHAT IS THE ORIGIN AND MEANING OF THE WORD SACRAMENT?

A. The Christian use of the word is based upon the old military use of the word which denotes the oath by which a soldier solemnly pledged obedience to his commander.

B. The Christian use of the word is also observed in the *Vulgate's* (a Latin version of the Scriptures made by Jerome at the close of the 4th century) use of it to translate the Greek word for mystery. The Sacraments were thus regarded as both pledges of obedience and as mysteries.

153. WHY DO SOME CHRISTIANS USE DIFFERENT TERMS?

A. In the Western Church these rites are called "Sacraments".

B. In the Eastern Orthodox Church they are called "Mysteries".

Some Protestants (because they feel that the other two words are colored with unhelpful associations) call these rites "ordinances".

Note!

The Scriptures allow us to classify these rites as signs and seals of our covenant relationship with God.

154. WHAT IS A GOOD WORKING DEFINITION OF A SACRAMENT?

A sacrament is a ritual action i.e., a formal customarily repeated act or series of acts instituted by Christ or the Church. It is perceived through the senses and sets forth to believers the grace of God in Christ and the blessings of His covenant. A sacrament moreover communicates, seals and confirms that a believer possesses certain New Covenant realities.

155. WHAT ARE THE COMPONENT PARTS OF A SACRAMENT THAT MUST BE DISTINGUISHED OR RECOGNIZED?

A. THE OUTWARD AND VISIBLE SIGN.

In the case of Water Baptism, it is the water and the act of being immersed into the water. In the case of the Lord's Supper, it is the ingesting of the bread and wine. In the case of Footwashing, it is the water and the act of washing the feet of a covenant brother or sister. *Where these elements are administered and appropriated, there (at that place) we have the entire external or outward and visible matter of the sacrament.* A person who receives only this outward and visible sign may be said to have received the sacrament, but he or she does not receive the whole or even the most important part of it. There is more.

B. THE INWARD SPIRITUAL GRACE

The sacraments are "holy signs and seals of the covenant of grace" (Rom. 4:11). A sign is something that points to something else. For instance, Abraham's circumcision pointed to and revealed "the righteousness of faith which he had while he was yet uncircumcised". **The sacrament of Water Baptism is a sign because it is an act that makes a declaration** of the saving grace of God in Christ Jesus.

Note!

The Saving Grace of God in Christ is thus distinguished from the sacrament which declares it.

156. WHAT ABOUT THE NUMBER OF SACRAMENTS? HOW MANY SACRAMENTS ARE THERE?

Historically the Church has recognized seven Sacraments of the New Covenant Church. They are as follows:

1. Water Baptism

2. Holy Communion or The Lord's Supper

3. Confirmation

4. Foot Washing

5. Matrimony

6. The Dedication of Children to God

7. The Anointing with Oil

157. WHO MAY RIGHTLY PARTICIPATE IN THE SACRAMENTS OF THE CHURCH?

The key to the correct answer to this question lies in the recognition that these are Sacraments (Sacred Acts) of the Covenant Community — The Church. Only those who are a part of the Covenant People of God may partake of the Sacraments.

158. HOW DO WE PREPARE OURSELVES FOR RECEIVING OR PARTICIPATING IN A SACRAMENT?

A. We prepare ourselves by studying and understanding what the Scriptures reveal about the particular Sacrament. By allowing the Holy Spirit to enlighten us in the Word, the way is cleared for a real experience with God.

Teaching them to observe all things whatsoever I have commanded you: and, lo, I am with you alway, even unto the end of the world. Amen.

Matthew 28:20

So then faith cometh by hearing, and hearing by the word of God.

Romans 10:17

B. We moreover clear the way for a real meeting with God by repentance and self examination. The Scriptures teach that the believer is responsible for judging himself on a continuous basis.

(1) The meaning and content of such self-judgment is well illustrated in the Old Testament book of Isaiah, Chapter 6:

- There is first of all the encounter with the Lord of glory, in whose light a true picture of the self is received (v. 1-4)

- Then there is the open confession of personal sin (vs. 5; I Jn. 1:7-9)

- Next there is the application of the cleansing ministry of the Father (vs. 6-7)

- Finally there is a restoration of divine human communication and the meaningful pursuit of a God-given task (vs. 8-9)

(2) The Scriptures moreover require that at certain specific times self-judgment is to be carried out:

- In connection with the observance of the Lord's Supper. (I Cor. 11:28-31)

- During times of sickness

- In the normal course of studying and feeding on the Word of God. (Ps. 119:9; Prov. 3:5-6; II Tim. 3:16f)

Note!

When the believer fails to judge or examine himself in light of the Bible, chastening results. Here it must be observed that the normal New Testament word group pertaining to chastening or chastisement always set forth the idea of "training", "discipline", and "correction". There are other words used that, when translated, tell us the undeniable positive purpose of God is moral improvement.

I Corinthians 11:28

We also prepare ourselves by asking God, in faith, to give us what He has promised and ordained for us in the Sacrament.

Hebrews 11:6

Luke 11:9-13

Finally, we prepare ourselves by willingly submitting ourselves to obey all that is commanded in the Sacrament — not mixing in any worldly tradition.

Mark 7:7-9

Matthew 15:3, 6

Colossians 2:8

Hebrews 8:5

Conclusion

We may now conclude this lesson by simply observing that two of the identifying marks of a New Covenant community are the faithful preaching of the Word of God, and the right use of the Sacraments. Ideally a local Christian congregation will exhibit other marks of its identity alongside these two. These additional marks are not, however, on the same level as the Word and the Sacraments. Through these channels, the grace of God is ministered to the Lord's People in a special way. Thank God for this amazing provision!

Lesson Twenty

Acts 14:21-25

21 And when they had preached the gospel to that city, and had taught many, they returned again to Lystra, and to Iconium, and Antioch,

22 Confirming the souls of the disciples, and exhorting them to continue in the faith, and that we must through much tribulation enter into the kingdom of God.

23 And when they had ordained them elders in every church, and had prayed with fasting, they commended them to the Lord, on whom they believed.

24 And after they had passed throughout Pisidia, they came to Pamphylia.

25 And when they had preached the word in Perga, they went down into Attalia:

Acts 15:32, 41

32 And Judas and Silas, being prophets also themselves, exhorted the brethren with many words, and confirmed them.

41 And he went through Syria and Cilicia, confirming the churches.

THE SACRAMENT OF CONFIRMATION

In the course of our Christian growth and development, as members of the Redeemed Community, we are expected (after we've been duly discipled) to make a mature public affirmation of faith and commitment to the Lord Jesus Christ and the New Covenant way of life. Once those who are over us in the Lord are convinced of our instruction in the principle doctrines of Christ, and of our confidence and trust in the Lord, then, we are to receive the laying on of hands by the Presbytery of Elders.

159. WHAT IS CONFIRMATION?

Confirmation is traditionally viewed as a sacrament of the Church. Through the laying on of the hands of the Elders or Presbytery, members of the Church are settled, strengthened and established in the faith of Jesus Christ. After being instructed in the Scriptures, believers who have experienced or who have properly laid the following foundation stones may be confirmed:

1. Repentance from Dead Works
2. Faith Toward God
3. Water Baptism
4. Baptism in the Holy Spirit
   (Acts 15:32,41; 14:11-22; I Pet. 5:10)

160. HOW IS CONFIRMATION ADMINISTERED?

The most effective method of confirming the saints is through the laying on of the hands of the Elders or Presbytery of the Church.

(Acts. 6:6; I Tim. 4:14)

161. IS IT REALLY NECESSARY FOR US TO BE CONFIRMED?

Yes! It is necessary for us to be established in the faith so we'll not be led astray by false doctrine and deceiving spirits.

(Zech. 10:12; II Thes. 3:3; Rom. 1:1; 12:2)

162. WHAT IS A GOOD SUMMARY OF THE BLESSINGS OF CONFIRMATION?

1. Confirmation strengthens, settles and establishes us in the faith.

2. Confirmation gives the believer new responsibilities in the local church and causes his ministry to be acknowledged by the congregation.

3. Often times the Holy Spirit will speak through the Presbytery and commission the believer to a particular ministry or calling.

4. Whenever a commission accompanies confirmation, spiritual gifts and graces may be imparted to the believer via the laying on of the hands of the Presbytery. (Ps. 68:9)

163. IS THERE MORE THAN ONE CONFIRMATION FOR BELIEVERS?

Yes! There are three kinds of confirmation which may be experienced one at a time.

1. General confirmation. This is to establish the believer in the faith (I Cor. 1:5-6; II Tim. 3:14)

2. Confirmation at the beginning of a ministry. (I Tim. 1:18; 4:14; II Tim. 1:6)

3. Confirmation at the time of ordination. (Acts 13:1-3)

164. HOW CAN STRENGTH, ESTABLISHMENT, SPIRITUAL GIFTS AND GRACES BE IMPARTED BY THE LAYING ON OF HANDS?

Through the Law of Contact and Transmission there is an impartation of the creative Spirit of God which strengthens and establishes the Saints. Spiritual gifts and ministries are spoken into being by the anointed Word of Prophecy.

> *This charge I commit unto thee, son Timothy, according to the prophecies which went before on thee, that thou by them mightest war a good warfare.*
>
> I Timothy 1:18

> *Neglect not the gift that is in thee, which was given thee by prophecy, with the laying on of the hands of the presbytery.*
>
> I Timothy 4:14

> *Quench not the Spirit.*
>
> *Despise not prophesyings.*

Prove all things; hold fast that which is good.

I Thessalonians 5:19-21

And they rose early in the morning, and went forth into the wilderness of Tekoa: and as they went forth, Jehoshaphat stood and said, Hear me, O Judah, and ye inhabitants of Jerusalem; Believe in the Lord your God, so shall ye be established; believe his prophets, so shall ye prosper.

II Chronicles 20:20

Conclusion

The scriptures teach that in the last days deceiving spirits and rebellion will run rampant throughout the land. One way of countering this demonic assault is to make sure that every member of the local church (especially those with a ministry calling upon their lives) is properly established in the present truth. This I what confirmation is all about.

Lesson Twenty-One

I Corinthians 11:23-26

23 For I have received of the Lord that which also I delivered unto you, That the Lord Jesus the same night in which he was betrayed took bread:

24 And when he had given thanks, he brake it, and said, Take, eat: this is my body, which is broken for you: this do in remembrance of me.

25 After the same manner also he took the cup, when he had supped, saying, This cup is the new testament in my blood: this do ye, as oft as ye drink it, in remembrance of me.

26 For as often as ye eat this bread, and drink this cup, ye do shew the Lord's death till he come.

THE SACRAMENT OF HOLY COMMUNION

On the night before He died, our Lord Jesus Christ instituted the Sacrament of Holy Communion. This ceremonial meal (also called "The Lord's Supper") confirmed the New Covenant made with the Father and fulfilled and replaced the Old Covenant Feast of the Passover.

We may safely say that no other visible institution of the Church impressed the mind and the imagination like the Lord's Supper; hence it becomes our duty to know what the Scriptures reveal about the nature of this institution. Let us attempt that duty prayerfully and in the power of the Holy Spirit.

165. WHAT IS HOLY COMMUNION?

By definition, Holy Communion is the sacred or Holy Act (meal) in which true Christians participate. Here the believer shares in a spiritual fellowship with other members of the Church and with the Lord Jesus Christ Himself.

> *The cup of blessing [of wine at the Lord's Supper] upon which we ask [God's] blessing, does it not mean [that in drinking it] we participate in and share a fellowship (a communion) in the blood of Christ, the Messiah? The bread which we break, does it not mean that in eating it] we participate in and share a fellowship (a communion) in the body of Christ? For we [no matter how] numerous we are,*

are one body, because we all partake of the one Bread [the One Whom the communion bread represents].

I Corinthians 10:16-17 (AMP)

In ancient times, eating a meal together had a special significance. In this way, Covenant relationship was expressed.

(Ex. 12:1-28; 24:9-11).

166. WHAT IS THE RELATIONSHIP BETWEEN THE PASSOVER OF THE OLD TESTAMENT AND THE HOLY COMMUNION OF THE NEW TESTAMENT?

A. The Passover Meal was an annual celebration in which Israel remembered their liberation from slavery in Africa. God's judgment came upon the Egyptians, and their firstborn children were slain. In order to escape this judgment every Israelite family was ordered as follows:

"Speak to all the congregation of Israel, saying: 'On the tenth of this month every man shall take for himself a lamb, according to the house of his father, a lamb for a household.

'Now you shall keep it until the fourteenth day of the same month. Then The whole assembly of the congregation of Israel shall kill it at twilight.

And they shall take some of the blood and put it on the two door posts and on the lintel of the houses where they eat it.

Then they shall eat the flesh on that night: roasted in the fire, with unleavened bread and with bitter herbs they shall eat it.

Exodus 12:3, 6-8 (NKJV)

And thus you shall eat it: with a belt on your waist, your sandals on your feet, and your staff in your hand. So you shall eat it in host. It is the Lord's Passover.

"For the Lord will pass through to strike the Egyptians; and when He sees the blood on the lintel and on the two doorposts, the Lord will pass over the door and not allow the destroyer to come into your houses to strike you.

Exodus 12:11, 23 (NKJV)

B. Holy Communion celebrates the time when our Lord, Jesus Christ became our Passover Lamb. He died for our sins. Actually, the Passover lamb of the Old Covenant was a sign, a type, and an example of the Lamb of God who would take away our sins.

The next day John seeth Jesus coming unto him, and saith, Behold the lamb of God, which taketh away the sin of the world.

John 1:29

Purge out therefore the old leaven, that ye may be a new lump, as ye are unleavened. For even Christ our passover is sacrificed for us:

I Corinthians 5:7

For as much as ye know that ye were not redeemed with corruptible things as silver and gold from your vain conversation received by tradition from your fathers;

But with the precious blood of Christ, as of a lamb without blemish and without spot:

I Peter 1:18-19

C. According to Matthew 26:26-27, Jesus instituted the New Covenant Meal on the same day as the Passover. This signified the Old Order had been fulfilled and replaced.

167. WHAT IS THE IMPORTANCE OF HOLY COMMUNION IN THE CHURCH? WHY DO WE CELEBRATE IT?

A. Note! When Holy Communion is observed in faith, we have real fellowship with the Great Head of the Church (the Lord Jesus Christ) and with the individual members of His Body — the Saints.

(I Cor. 10:1647 [AMP])

B. We celebrate the Lord's Supper for several reasons:

(1) Because Jesus commanded us to do it.

After the same manner also he took the cup when he had supped, saying This cup is the new testament in my blood: this do ye, as oft as ye drink it, in remembrance of me.

I Corinthians 11:25

(2) To experience the real presence and life of Christ in us.

I am the living bread which came down from heaven; if any man eat of this bread, he shall live forever: and the bread that I will give is my flesh, which I will give for the life of the world.

> *Then Jesus said unto them, Verily, verily, I say unto you, Except ye eat the flesh of the Son of man, and drink his blood, ye have no life in you.*
>
> John 6:51, 53

> *And he took bread, and gave thanks, and brake it, and gave unto them, saying, This is my body which is given for you; this do in remembrance of me.*
>
> Luke 22:19

(3) To have health

> *For he that eateth and drinketh unworthily, eateth and drinketh damnation to himself not discerning the Lord's body.*
>
> *For this cause many are weak and sickly among you and many sleep.*
>
> I Corinthians 11:29-30

(4) To remind us of the sacrifice of Jesus Christ for our redemption. (I Cor. 11:25)

> *And it shall come to pass, when your children shall say unto you, What mean ye by this service?*
>
> *That ye shall say, It is the sacrifice of the Lord's passover, who passed over the houses of the children of Israel in Egypt, when he smote the Egyptians, and delivered our houses. And the people bowed the head and worshipped.*
>
> Exodus 12:26-27

168. IN THE HOLY COMMUNION, WHAT DO WE EAT AND DRINK AS WE REMEMBER THE BROKEN

BODY AND THE SHED BLOOD OF OUR LORD JESUS CHRIST?

In remembrance of the broken body of our Lord Jesus Christ we eat bread. In remembrance of His shed blood, we drink the fruit of the vine — either grape juice or wine.

And as they did eat, Jesus took bread, and blessed, and brake it, and gave to them, and said, Take, eat: this is my body.

And he took the cup, and when he had given thanks, he gave it to them: they all drank of it.

And he said unto them, This is my blood of the new testament, which is shed for many.

Verily I say unto you, I will drink no more of the fruit of the vine, until that day that I drink it new in the kingdom of God.

Mark 14:22-25

169. WHAT ABOUT THE ORDER OF COMMUNION? DOES THE BIBLE TEACH ANY SPECIFIC PROCEDURE?

Yes! The example given by our Lord Jesus Christ in the last supper with his disciples reveals a pattern:

A. Jesus took bread

B. and blessed it

C. and brake it

D. and gave it to the disciples and said take eat. This is my body, and He took the cup and gave thanks, and gave it to them saying, drink ye all of it; for this is my blood

of the New Covenant which is shed for many for the remission of sins.
(Mt. 26:26-28)

170. CONCERNING THIS "DIVINE ORDER", DID JESUS TEACH IT DURING HIS EARTHLY MINISTRY?

A. When he performed the miracle with the loaves and the fishes, Jesus taught this "Divine Order".

And he commanded the multitude to sit down on the grass, and took the five loaves and the two fishes, and looking up to heaven, he blessed, and brake, and gave the loaves to his disciples, and the disciples to the multitude:

And they did all eat, and were filled: and they took up the fragments that remained twelve baskets full.

Matthew 14:19-20

B. Jesus revealed Himself to His disciples after the resurrection by the "breaking of bread" in this "Divine Order".

And it came to pass, as he sat at meat with them, he took bread and blessed it, and brake, and gave to them

And their eyes were opened, and they knew him; and he vanished out of their sight.

Luke 24:30-31

Note! In the same way that it was so important that the Ark of the Covenant be brought back to its proper place by following the "Due Order", so also our participation in the Lord's Supper must be "after the Due Order".

171. HOW OFTEN SHOULD THE CHURCH BREAK BREAD TOGETHER IN HOLY COMMUNION?

Actually, there are no clear instructions in the New Testament telling us how often we are to take communion. The earliest churches may have observed it every week. What we do know is that the Apostle Paul told the Corinthian Saints, "for as often as ye eat this bread and drink this cup…"

We recommend that the Holy Communion be celebrated at least once per month.

172. CAN ANYONE TAKE PART IN THE SACRAMENT OF HOLY COMMUNION?

No! The Lord's Supper is not for sinners (the unsaved). Only true believers who are in Covenant with the Lord Jesus Christ and His Church should take part.

> *In that ye have brought unto my sanctuary strangers, uncircumcised in heart, and uncircumcised in flesh, to be in my sanctuary, to pollute it, even my house, when ye offer my bread, the fat and the blood, and they have broken my covenant because of all your abominations.*
>
> Ezekiel 44:7

173. HOW DO WE PREPARE FOR HOLY COMMUNION?

A. The Scriptures are clear on this subject. We must examine our attitude and life to make sure that things are right between us and our covenant brothers and sisters, and between us and God. It is not our responsibility to judge and examine others!

Wherefore whosoever shall eat this bread, and drink this cup of the Lord, unworthily, shall be guilty of the body and blood of the Lord.

But let a man examine himself, and so let him eat of that bread, and drink of that cup.

For he that eateth and drinketh unworthily, eateth and drinketh damnation to himself, not discerning the Lord's body.

I Corinthians 11:27-29

B. As we thus examine ourselves, the Ten Commandments and the Standards and Values of the Church will prove to be helpful. Review these forms often.

C. Ask the Holy Spirit to help us recall sins for which we need to repent and then obey I John 1:7-9.

D. Make restitution wherever it's possible and purpose not to sin again.

Conclusion

We should never dodge communion; but rather, we should deal with our sins and bad relationships. Then, after making things right, go ahead and participate in the real presence and life of Jesus Christ, our Lord.

Lesson Twenty-Two

John 13:2-9

2 And supper being ended, the devil having now put into the heart of Judas Iscariot, Simon's son, to betray him;

3 Jesus knowing that the Father had given all things into his hands, and that he was come from God, and went to God;

4 He riseth from supper, and laid aside his garments; and took a towel, and girded himself.

5 After that he poureth water into a bason, and began to wash the disciples' feet, and to wipe them with the towel wherewith he was girded.

6 Then cometh he to Simon Peter: and Peter saith unto him, Lord, dost thou wash my feet?

7 Jesus answered and said unto him, What I do thou knowest not now; but thou shalt know hereafter.

8 Peter saith unto him, Thou shalt never wash my feet. Jesus answered him, If I wash thee not, thou hast no part with me.

9 Simon Peter saith unto him, Lord, not my feet only, but also my hands and my head.

The Sacrament of Foot Washing

In the thirteenth chapter of the Gospel of John, Jesus initiated the Sacrament of Foot Washing. This holy event effectively deals with the enmity that often frustrates the fellowship between Covenant brothers and sisters. Jesus desires that all of His people experience this great occasion.

> *The evening meal was being served, and the devil had already prompted Judas Iscariot, son of Simon, to betray Jesus. 'Jesus knew that the Father had put all things under his power, and that he had come from God and was returning to God; "so he got up from the meal, took off his outer clothing, and wrapped a towel around his waist. 'After that, he poured water into a basin and began to wash his disciples' feet, drying them with the towel that was wrapped around him.*
>
> *He came to Simon Peter, who said to him, "Lord, are you going to wash my feet?"*
>
> *Jesus replied, "You do not realize now what I am doing: but later you will understand."*
>
> *"No," said Peter, "you shall never wash my feet." Jesus answered, "Unless I wash you, you have no part with me."*
>
> *"Then, Lord," Simon Peter replied, "not just my feet but my hands and my head as well!"*
>
> John 13:2-9 (NIV)

174. WHAT IS FOOT WASHING?

Unfortunately, many Christians think that washing the Saint's feet is no more than a customary act of hospitality for Jesus' day, but not an ordinance to be observed in this present time. Actually, the New Testament teaches that foot washing was instituted by the Lord Jesus Christ as a practical means by which we (believers) may fulfill the commandment to love our neighbors (Covenant brothers and sisters) as we love ourselves.

> *If I then, your Lord and Teacher (Master), have washed your feet, you ought [it is your duty, you are under obligation, you owe it] to wash one another's feet.*
>
> *For I have given you this as an example, so that you should do [in your turn] what I have done to you.*
>
> John 13:14-15 (AMP)

175. CAN WE PROVE THAT THE PRACTICE OF FOOT WASHING IS MORE THAN AN ANCIENT CUSTOM OR MORE THAN A SHOW OF HOSPITALITY?

Yes! There are several facts which prove that foot washing was (and is) more than an old custom that expressed hospitality. Read John 13:2-9 and observe:

A. It was customary to offer a guest a basin of water to wash his feet when he entered a home; however, in the text the timing was very unusual for Jesus to wash the disciples' feet (at the supper table) unless He intended to teach them a spiritual lesson.

B. The Old Testament Scriptures reveal that, even when it was an act of hospitality, the guests washed their own feet.

Note! In Genesis 18:2-4 and 19:1-2, both the angels and the Lord were invited to wash their own feet.

C. In vs. 7, Peter would surely have known what Jesus was doing if it had been a mere social custom.

D. According to the text, Jesus performed this act upon men whose feet were already clean. They could have said to Him, "Lord, our feet are already clean. Why are you washing us? Obviously, it must have been a symbolic washing with a spiritual meaning.

E. Jesus revealed that the washing of their feet was essential for fellowship with Him. His strong rebuke in vs. 8 moved Peter (immediately) to obedience, even though he did not really know all that Jesus meant.

F. The crowning proof that foot washing was not just an act of hospitality or a custom can be seen in I Timothy 5:9-10. Here the Apostle Paul requires that any widow who is to be supported by the Church must meet several qualifications.

Do not let a widow under sixty years old be taken into the number, and not unless she has been the wife of one man,

well reported for good works; if she has brought up children, if she has lodged strangers, if she has washed the saints' feet, if she has relieved the afflicted, if she has diligently followed every good work.

I Timothy 5:9-10 (NKJV)

Note how the Apostle makes a difference between her treatment of the Saints, and her treatment of strangers. She showed hospitality to the strangers; but, in contrast, she extended her love to the saints by washing their feet.

176. WHAT THEN, IS THE REAL MEANING OF THE SACRAMENT OF FOOT WASHING?

A. By washing the disciple's feet, Jesus demonstrated the self-abasing kind of humility and brotherly love that the Church must display now in the midst of this crooked and perverse generation.
(Mt. 19:19; Rom. 12:9-21)

B. The story of the woman who washed Jesus' feet with her tears expressed the real meaning of the Sacrament of Foot Washing.
Luke 7:36-50 (NKJV)

Note! A socially unacceptable woman who was a great sinner (one who had been forgiven much) demonstrated much love and humility. So must we. The net result of all of this is stated in the words of Jesus: "Then said Jesus to the woman, your faith has saved you. Go in peace."

C. Foot washing occasions the removal of the enmity (hatred, hostility or ill-will) that from time to time arises between Covenant brothers and sisters. The removal of this enmity enables us to love as Jesus loved
(Jn. 15:12-13; Eph. 4:32; 5:25; Col. 3:13).

177. EXPLAIN THIS ENMITY THAT FROM TIME TO TIME ARISES BETWEEN COVENANT BROTHERS AND SISTERS. WHAT IS IT?

Actually, this enmity or hostility is no more than our inner desire to rule over others. It is our determination to walk in pride and to seek after our own interests at the expense of others.

> *For I say, through the grace given unto me, to every man that is among you, not to think of himself more highly than he ought to think; but to think soberly, according as God hath dealt to every man the measure of faith.*
> Romans 12:3

178. WHAT'S SO BAD ABOUT THIS ENMITY OR HOSTILITY TOWARD OUR COVENANT BROTHERS AND SISTERS?

Proverbs 16:18

Daniel 5:20-21

Luke 22:24-27

Luke 14:11

These Scriptural references teach that enmity between Covenant people leads to ruin. Neither the individual Christian nor the local community of Christians benefit when such ill-will prevails.

179. DO THE SCRIPTURES TEACH THAT FOOT WASHING ALONE WILL STRAIGHTEN OUT THE RELATIONAL PROBLEMS BETWEEN THE SAINTS?

No! Matthew 18:15-17 and I John 1:7-9 may need to be applied in order for the root causes of hostility to be removed.

180. WHAT IS THE BEST WAY FOR US TO PREPARE FOR OBSERVING THE SACRAMENT OF FOOT WASHING?

By genuine repentance and by obeying God's Word we prepare for the sacrament.

8 Draw nigh to God, and he will draw night to you, Cleanse your hands, ye sinners; and purify your hearts, ye double-minded.

9 Be afflicted, and mourn, and weep: let your laughter be turned to mourning and your joy to heaviness.

10 Humble yourselves in the sight of the Lord, and he shall lift you up.

James 4:8-10

181. WHAT ABOUT THE PROCEDURE? WHAT IS THE PROPER WAY TO DO IT?

Note! Jesus gives us the best example.

He riseth from supper, and laid aside his garments; and took a towel, and girded himself

After that he poureth water into a basin and began to wash the disciples' feet, and to wipe them with the towel wherewith he was girded.

John 13:4-5

The men and the women should be separated into different groups. Men are to wash men's feet and women are to wash women's feet.

Let all things be done decently and in order.

I Corinthians 14:40

It is important to see here that when we wash the feet of our covenant brothers and sisters a much needed humbling takes place in us. At the same time our spiritual sense comes to the surface and we rejoice in the truth that our covenant friend is actually made in God's image and likeness.

Moreover, when a covenant brother or sister washes our feet, we learn (by experience) how important it is that we receive the positive love expressions that Christ ministers to us in the sacrament. This is not always easy; but, the words of Jesus will be helpful:

6 Then cometh he to Simon Peter: and Peter saith unto him, Lord, dost thou wash my feet?

7 Jesus answered and said unto him, What I do thou knowest not now; but thou shalt know hereafter.

8 Peter saith unto him, Thou shalt never wash my feet. Jesus answered him, If I wash thee not, thou hast no part with me.

John 13:6-8

Conclusion

All in all, footwashing is a practical way of developing humility and a servant attitude. It is also a good way of making sure that we do not think of ourselves more highly than we ought to think.

Lesson Twenty-Three

Ephesians 5:31-33

31 For this cause shall a man leave his father and mother, and shall be joined unto his wife, and they two shall be one flesh.

32 This is a great mystery: but I speak concerning Christ and the church.

33 Nevertheless let every one of you in particular so love his wife even as himself; and the wife see that she reverence her husband.

The Sacrament of Matrimony

The Sacrament of Matrimony or marriage is important for the life of mankind in general and the life of the Church in particular. It is a holy event and it is ordained by God. Through it a man and a woman are united together in covenant and given grace to bless the union and to make it whole and spiritual.

182. WHAT IS HOLY MATRIMONY?

Holy Matrimony is a sacred covenant instituted by God in which a man and a woman enter into a lifelong union by vows or oaths made to each other in the presence of God.

(Mt. 19:4-6)

183. HOW IMPORTANT IS MARRIAGE AND THE FAMILY?

Marriage (and the family) is the God-ordained place for the establishment and the development of the following:

A. Right relationship and fellowship. (Gen. 2:28)

B. God-like character.

(Gal. 5:22-23; II Pet. 1:3ff; I Cor 7:9)

C. God-ordained ministry and function. (Gen. 1:28-29)

D. Natural and spiritual reproduction. (Gen. 1:28)

184. WHAT IS THE NATURE OF THE AGREEMENT MADE IN THE MARRIAGE COVENANT?

Both the husband and wife agree to:

A. Live together after God's ordinance.

B. Love, comfort, honor and care for each other.

C. Forsake all others.

D. Commit themselves to each other for life.

For this cause shall a man leave his father and mother, and shall be joined unto his wife, and they two shall be one flesh.

This is a great mystery: but I speak concerning Christ and the church.

Nevertheless let every one of you in particular so love his wife even as himself; and the wife see that she reverence her husband.

Ephesians 5:31-33

"The intention of marriage is that one husband should have one wife, and one wife should have one husband (at a time). Marriage is thus God's gift for the preservation of man's health in this world and for his salvation in the world to come."

The Ethiopian Tewahedo Church (an integrally African Church), Archbishop Yesehaq, p. 115,

James C. Winston Publishing Co., Inc.

185. WHAT DOES UNITY HAVE TO DO WITH THE FULFILLMENT OF GOD'S PURPOSE FOR MARRIAGE AND THE FAMILY?

God's purpose here is fulfilled when unity is achieved. Read Genesis 2:24 and Matthew 19:5-6. The King James Version says, "they shall be (or become) one". This implies a process and not a crisis experience.

  A. Oneness in spirit is brought about by family worship "in spirit and in truth".

(Jn. 4:24)

  B. Oneness of soul is brought about by communicating, talking together and fellowshipping. The Bible highlights a special kind of relationship that we call a "soul tie". A soul tie is a strong bond between two people in the realm of the soul (reason, emotions and will). An example of a good soul tie between friends is seen in the story of Jonathan and David in I Samuel 18:1. Their souls were knit together in a bond that was pure and not polluted by any selfish desire. This same kind of self-sacrificing soul tie is observed in the lives of Ruth and Naomi. Good marriages are based upon these deep, soulish ties that provide emotional and mental strength in times of adversity and a reason to rejoice together in times of triumph.

  C. Oneness of body is effected or brought about through physical love and affection between husband and wife.

Note! If the husband and the wife have the right spiritual attitudes, then, they will both be able to achieve the kind of unity or oneness that God requires. Study Ephesians 5:18-21 and observe the following commands:

- "Be filled with the Holy Spirit"
- "Speak to one another in psalms and hymns and spiritual songs.
- "Make melody in your hearts to the Lord."
- Give thanks always in the Name of the Lord Jesus Christ."
- "Submit yourselves to one another in the fear of Christ."

These are attitudes that make for real unity in a Christian marriage and family.

186. ARE THERE ANY TERMS OR CONDITIONS GIVEN IN THE SCRIPTURES THAT WE MUST OBEY?

Yes! God has set down several such terms or conditions for Christian marriage.

    A. It is God's will that believers marry only believers.

Be ye not unequally yoked together with unbelievers: for what fellowship hast righteousness with unrighteousness? and what communion hath light with darkness?

And what concord hath Christ with Belial? or what part hath he that believeth with an infidel?

And what agreement hath the temple of God with idols? for ye are the temple of the living God as God hath said, I will dwell in them, and walk in them; and I will be their God, and they shall be my people.

II Corinthians 6:14-16

"A woman is bound to her husband as long as he lives. But if her husband dies, she is free to marry anyone she wishes, but he must belong to the Lord.

I Corinthians 7:39 (NIV)

Observe! When a spouse becomes saved, his or her union with the unsaved spouse is still sacred in the sight of God.

(I Cor. 7:12-14)

B. God forbids premarital and extramarital sexual relations. Why? Because these illicit relations portray a spiritual union or marriage covenant that really does not exist, and therefore, they perpetrate a lie. Moreover, adultery violates one's pledge of exclusive love to his or her spouse.

C. The sexual relationship in marriage is not evil and shameful, but holy, pleasurable and purposeful. It expresses the deep meaning and quality of the love relationship between a husband and his wife. It also promotes growth and mutual understanding.

(Eph. 5:3-5, I Thes. 4:3-7; I Cor. 6:15-18)

Marriage should be honored by all, and the marriage bed kept pure, for God will judge the adulterer and all the sexually immoral.

Hebrews 14:4 (NIV)

D. Christians are not to marry anyone who has been divorced unless the previous marriage covenant has been dissolved according to Biblical standards.

"It has been said, 'Anyone who divorces his wife must give her a certificate of divorce.' But I tell you that anyone who divorces his wife, except for marital unfaithfulness, causes her to become an adulteress and anyone who marries the divorced woman commits adultery."

Matthew 5:31-32 (NIV)

Romans 7:2-3

Matthew 19:39

Note! In this last text Jesus recognizes that sexual immorality ("porneia") potentially destroys the marriage covenant between spouses and is therefore grounds for legal divorce; however, divorce is not mandatory! Reconciliation is preferable.

(Mt. 18:21-35)

E. The husband and the wife must recognize that in Christ both are equal as persons and have the same standing. (I Cor. 7:4;11:11-12; Gal. 3:28)

Moreover, they must see that God's social order for mankind calls for male headship in the home and in the local church.

(Eph. 5:22-23; I Cor. 14:34; 1 Tim. 2:11-42)

When God's order is honored, it brings His blessings. When it is ignored, it incurs trouble and unhappiness.

187. WHAT IS THE WIFE'S RELATIONSHIP TO HER HUSBAND?

A. Study Eph. 5:22-27; Col. 3:18-21; I Pet. 3:1-6.

B. In Genesis 3:16b the words, "Your desire shall be for your husband" are better tanslated, "your desire shall be to dominate or 'Lord it over' your husband".

C. The words, "and he shall rule over you" are not intended to reduce a woman's personhood or giftedness; rather, they are intended to show that God desired to reinstate the original partnership of the husband and the wife in ministry. There is no male dominance over females here; however it does assign husbandly responsibility for leadership in the marriage relationship.

D. According to Titus 2:3-5 and Ephesians 5:33, wives must reverence and love their husbands.

188. WHAT IS THE HUSBAND'S RELATIONSHIP TO HIS WIFE?

Here again, the relationship of the husband to his wife is a demonstration of Christ's relationship to the Church.

(I Cor. 11:3-12; Eph. 5:23-29; I Pet. 3:7)

A. The husband is the head or "covering" of his wife:

   1. He directs.

   2. He protects.

   3. He interprets her reactions.

B. The husband is commanded to LOVE, whereas the wife is commanded to submit.

C. The husband should be instrumental in moving his wife along into God's purpose.
(Eph. 5:26-27)

189. IS THERE A PICTURE IN THE SCRIPTURES OF A GOOD HUSBAND?

Yes! The Lord Jesus Christ is set forth in the Bible as our example of a good husband. He models all of the character traits that Christian wives have a right to expect in their husbands:

A. Love and compassion

B. Patience

C. Consideration

D. Understanding

E. Willingness to "lay down" his life for his beloved

Study Ephesians 5:23, 25-31 in three different modern versions.

190. WHAT ARE SOME GOOD CONFESSIONS FOR THE CHRISTIAN MARRIAGE, WIFE AND HUSBAND?

A. Confessions for the marriage:

Our Father in Heaven, we come before You in the Name of Jesus. It is to be recorded in Heaven, on earth, and beneath the earth that we, Your children, shall give ourselves continually to prayer and the ministry of Your Word, and that we will not let any corrupt communication proceed out of our mouths, but our words shall edify, build up, comfort, and minister grace unto each other.

We will always be kind to each other, tenderhearted and always forgiving. We confess now that we will always be moved with compassion and love will direct our life.

We will always be found and known to speak the words of our Father, for they are Spirit and they are life. We will live by Your Word, will be willing and obedient and will walk in the light of what we know.

We will endeavor to keep the unity of the Spirit in the bond of peace. We will stand fast, no matter the cost.

We are the light of the world, workmen that needeth not to be ashamed. For God's Word says if we will cleanse ourselves from what is common, we will become vessels for noble use, set apart for use even to the Master of the house and yes, fit for any good purpose.

We bring our body under subjection to the Word, for our body is the temple of the Lord.

We praise You, Father, and worship You, for our faith shall never fail, for we will always operate in love and we will always be found spreading the Word and doing the works of our Father.

B. Confessions for the Wife:

Phil. 1:6 Being confident that He who began a good work in me will continue until the day of Jesus Christ, I confess that:

Prov. 31:10 I am a capable, intelligent and virtuous woman, far more precious than jewels.

Prov. 31:15 I rise early and get spiritual food for my household.

Matt. 6:33 I seek first God's Kingdom and all good things are added unto me.

Prov. 31:30-31 I reverently and worshipfully fear the Lord.

Prov. 31:13 I give of the fruit of my hands and my works praise me. I am industrious.

Prov. 31:16 With my savings I plant fruitful vines.

Prov. 31:25 Strength and dignity are my clothing and my position is strong and secure. I rejoice over the future knowing that my family and I are in readiness for it.

Prov. 31:26 I open my mouth with skillful and godly wisdom, and in my tongue is the law of kindness, giving counsel and instruction.

Prov. 31:27 The bread of idleness (gossip, discontent and self-pity) I do not eat.

I Tim. 3:11 I am worthy of respect and serious, not a gossiper, but temperate and self-controlled, thoroughly trustworthy in all things.

I Tim. 6:11 I pursue righteousness, godliness, faith, love

Neh. 8:10 patience and gentleheartedness, and the joy of the Lord is my strength.

Eph. 5:22 I am submissive and adapt myself to my own husband as a service to the Lord. He is head

Eph. 5:23 of me as Christ is head of the Church.

Eph. 5:33 I respect and reverence my husband. I notice, regard, honor, prefer, love and admire him exceedingly.

Prov. 31:11 The heart of my husband does trust in me confidently and relies on and believes in me safely.

Prov. 31:12 I comfort and encourage and do him only good as long as there is life in me. I walk in

Eph. 5:2 love with my husband, esteeming and delighting in him.

Prov. 31:29 My husband praises me above all women.

C. Confessions for the Husband:

Josh. 24:15 I have chosen this day whom I will serve; as for me and my household, we will serve the Lord.

Deut. 30:19-20 I choose the blessing of life that I and my descendants may live; to love the Lord our God, to obey His voice and to cling to Him; for He is our life, and the length of our days.

Ps. 91:1 I dwell in the secret place of the Most High. I remain stable and fixed under the shadow of the Almighty. Because the Lord is my refuge and the Most High my dwelling place, no evil shall befall me nor any plague or calamity come near my family or home.

Deut 29:9 Because I abide in the Word, I deal wisely and prosper in all that I do.

Eph. 3:17 Because I am rooted and grounded in love,

Eph. 4:2; 5:2 I forbear others in love and walk in love.

Eph. 5:23-25 As Christ is the head of the Church, I am head of my wife and responsible to and for her.

Col. 3:19 I love my wife. I am affectionate and sympathetic with her. I nourish, carefully protect and cherish her. I am willing to give up all for her.

1 Pet. 3:7 Because I live considerately with my wife, honoring her as the weaker vessel, and realizing we are joint heirs of the grace of life, my prayers are not hindered.

Eph. 5:31 My wife and I have

Gen. 2:24 become one body, one flesh.

Col 2:2 Our hearts are knit together in love.

Rom. 14:19 We follow after the things which make for peace,

II Cor. 13:11 and things which edify each other.

II Tim. 2:22 We live in peace and follow after peace, because

Col. 3:15 the peace of God rules in our hearts.

 Conclusion

There's no feeling in the world comparable to that which comes with loving a person and then having that love returned. Loving another person is something that God created us for. He decided to mold us in such a way that we could love another individually, exclusively, deeply and devotedly for the rest of our lives. This is amazing!

When the Lord presented Eve to Adam, he was evidently pleased and excited about his gorgeous gift. He exclaimed:

"This is now bone of my bones

And flesh of my flesh;

She shall be called Woman,

Because she was taken out of Man."

Therefore a man shall leave his father and mother and be joined to his wife, and they shall become one flesh.

Genesis 2:23-24 (NKJV)

This meant that at an important juncture in life, both the priorities and the status of a man and a woman will change. Whenever this happens, they must be prepared not only to leave the single life, but to moreover commit themselves to the covenant of marriage as well. At the marriage altar they will publicly set their affections upon one another and keep them there throughout the many ups and downs of life. This is the way Jesus loves us, and this is the way He would have us love each other.

Lesson Twenty-Four

Mark 10:13-16

13 And they brought young children to him, that he should touch them: and his disciples rebuked those that brought them.

14 But when Jesus saw it, he was much displeased, and said unto them, Suffer the little children to come unto me, and forbid them not: for of such is the kingdom of God.

15 Verily I say unto you, Whosoever shall not receive the kingdom of God as a little child, he shall not enter therein.

16 And he took them up in his arms, put his hands upon them, and blessed them.

THE SACRAMENT OF THE DEDICATION OF CHILDREN

Christian parents have a covenant obligation to give their children godly instruction and correction. Why? Because the children of the saints are special to the Lord, and must be prepared to live a life that's pleasing to Him (Mal. 2:15).

191. WHAT IS THE FIRST STEP TOWARD PREPARING OUR CHILDREN FOR THE LIFE THAT PLEASES GOD?

The first thing Christian parents should do to prepare their children for the life that pleases God is to dedicate them to the Lord at the very beginning of their lives. A Christian father and mother should have no problem bringing their children to the Lord in order that they may be blessed.

> *When the time of their purification according to the Law of Moses had been completed, Joseph and Mary took him to Jerusalem to present him to the Lord*
>
> *(as it is written in the Law of the Lord, "Every firstborn male is to be consecrated to the Lord"), and to offer a sacrifice in keeping with what is said in the Law of the Lord...*
>
> Luke 2:22-24

192. MORE SPECIFICALLY, WHAT IS THE SACRAMENT OF THE DEDICATION OF CHILDREN?

The Sacrament of the Dedication of Children is a sacred event in which saved parents present their children unto God so that the purpose of the Lord may be fulfilled in them.

27 For this child I prayed; and the Lord hath given me my petition which I asked of him:

28 Therefore also I have lent him to the Lord; as long as he liveth he shall be lent to the Lord. And he worshipped the Lord there.

1 Sam 1:27:28

16 And he took them up in his arms, put his hands upon them, and blessed them.

Mark 10:16

Actually, dedication is synonymous with sanctification (which has to do with the setting apart of a person or a thing for a sacred or holy use). The Apostle Paul explains that children (under the New Covenant) can be set into a special place of privilege and blessing before the Lord. How? By the Covenant standing of the saved parent(s).

14 For the unbelieving husband is sanctified by the wife, and the unbelieving wife is sanctified by the husband: else were your children unclean; but now are they holy.

I Corinthians 7:14

The Sacrament of the Dedication of Children is a holy occasion wherein children of saved parents (or a saved parent) are actually set apart unto God to participate in the blessings of the Covenant.

193. IN DEDICATING THEIR CHILDREN TO GOD, WHAT SPECIFIC RESPONSIBILITIES FALL UPON CHRISTIAN PARENTS?

Note! Christian parents should:

A. Teach their children to fear (to reverence and to stand in awe of) the Lord and to turn away from sin and evil.

(Heb. 1:9)

B. Teach their children to obey their parents through Biblical discipline.

(Dt. 8:5; Prov. 3:11-12;13:24;23:13-14;29:15, 17; Col. 3:20-21)

C. Protect their children from ungodly influences.

(Prov. 13:20; 28:7; I Jn. 2:15-17)

D. Lead their children into a saving knowledge of the Lord Jesus Christ.

(Mt. 19:14; Prov. 22:6; Ecc. 12:1)

E. Make sure that the family is established in a local church where the Lord Jesus Christ and the Scriptures are honored, and where the Holy Spirit and His gifts are in real manifestation.

(Ps. 19:63; Acts 1:4-5, 8; 2:4,39, 42-47).

F. Encourage their children (by precept and example) to be separated from the world and to witness and work for the Lord

(II Cor. 6:14-18; Jas. 4:4; Heb 11:13-16; Phil. 3:20, Col. 3:1-3)

G. Teach their children to pray.

(Acts 6:4; Rom. 12:12; Eph. 6:18; Jas. 5:16)

H. Teach their Children the Holy Commandments of God and the story of His Mighty Redemption.

(Deut. 6:4-28; Gal.3)

I. Pray for their Children, using Ephesians 1:15-23 as a model:

Dear Lord,

I thank and praise you for my son/daughter, (name) and I now ask you, the God and Father of our Lord Jesus Christ, to give unto him/her the spirit of wisdom and revelation that he/she may know you better. I pray that the eyes of (name) spirit would be enlightened so that he/she may know the hope to which God has called him/her, what God is getting when He gets us, and the exceeding greatness of His power and ability toward us who believe.

Parents should promise to fulfill the nine specific responsibilities listed above and to support each other in the achievement of this goal by their own prayers and witness.

194. HOW DO GODPARENTS FIGURE INTO ALL OF THIS?

Godparents are honored to be included as "members of the family" and as such, occupy a position of trust. Their job is to help their Godchild to grow up whole and strong. This implies a spiritual relationship to the child and to his or her development that is both deep and holy.

The Godparents should also promise to help fulfill the nine specific responsibilities that fall upon the Christian parents.

195. IS THERE ANY KIND OF PREPARATION OR TRAINING FOR GODPARENTS?

Yes! Children learn most from the lifestyle or example of those close to them. Godparents (along with the parents) should therefore review and reaffirm their own commitment to the following:

COVENANT OF FAITH

Beloved in Christ Jesus, our Lord, you have learned that the Dedication of Children is a Sacrament of the Church that's intended to seal unto us and our seed the blessings of God's Covenant; therefore, that it may be revealed that you are thus minded, you are to answer sincerely to these questions:

Do you believe in God the Father?

Response: I believe in God the Father Almighty, Creator of heaven and earth.

Do you believe in Jesus Christ the Son of the Living God?

Response: I believe in Jesus Christ, the only begotten Son of the Living God and our Lord.

Do you believe in His virgin birth?

Response: I believe in the virgin birth of our Lord Jesus Christ who was conceived by the Holy Ghost and born of the Virgin Mary.

Do you believe in the death and burial of Jesus Christ?

Response: I believe that our Lord Jesus Christ suffered under Pontius Pilate, was crucified, died and was buried.

Do you believe in the resurrection of Jesus Christ from the dead?

Response: Yes, I believe that Jesus Christ after he was buried descended into hell and on the third day he arose from the dead.

Do you believe Jesus Christ is now in heaven with God the Father?

Response: I believe Jesus Christ ascended into heaven and now sits on the right hand of God, the Father Almighty.

Do you believe Jesus Christ will return to judge the living and the dead?

Response: Yes, I believe that Jesus Christ shall return from heaven to judge the living and the dead.

Do you believe the Bible is the inspired Word of God?

Response: I do believe the Bible is the inspired Word of God and was written by holy men of God as they were moved by the Holy Ghost.

Do you believe the Bible is the only standard for faith and practice?

Response: Yes, I believe the Bible is the only standard for faith and practice. Therefore I will live my life according to the precepts and doctrine found therein.

196. WHAT ABOUT THE ACTUAL PRESENTATION OF THE CHILDREN FOR DEDICATION? HOW SHOULD THIS BE DONE?

Parents and Godparents should present their children individually as follows:

We, the parents and Godparents, of (name) do now in the presence of God and this fellowship of believers present (name) to receive the Sacrament of the Dedication of Children.

(After presenting the children, the minister asks the parents and Godparents:)

Do you acknowledge that your children are sanctified or set apart unto the blessings of the Lord by your position as a born-again parent?

Response: Yes! We do acknowledge this truth.

Do you also acknowledge the doctrines of the New Covenant and the articles of the Christian faith which are taught here in this local church to be the truth of God unto salvation to all who believe?

Response: Yes! We do acknowledge and believe this truth.

Finally, do you promise and take upon yourself the responsibility for seeing that the child you are now presenting is brought up in the nurture and the admonition of Jesus Christ?

Response: We will, by the help of the Lord!

(At this point the minister should pray a prayer of dedication and pronounce the blessings of God upon the candidate(s), the parents and Godparents)

Conclusion

The Sacrament of the Dedication of Children is more than sprinkling children with holy water or anointing them with holy oil. It is making a promise to God i.e., a covenant with God to bring up our children in a Christian family and to instruct them in God's Word. It moreover, involves living a godly life before our children on a daily basis.

Lesson Twenty-Five

Exodus 28:41

41 And thou shalt put them upon Aaron thy brother, and his sons with him; and shalt anoint them, and consecrate them, and sanctify them, that they may minister unto me in the priest's office.

Matthew 6:17

17 But thou, when thou fastest, anoint thine head, and wash thy face;

James 5:14

14 Is any sick among you? let him call for the elders of the church; and let them pray over him, anointing him with oil in the name of the Lord:

The Sacrament of Anointing with Oil

The anointing with oil is referred to throughout the Scriptures. In Ruth it was used as a cosmetic; in II Chronicles 28:15 it was used for refreshing the body; in Esther 2:12 and Isaiah 57:9 it was used for purifying the body; in Isaiah 1:6; Mark 6:13; Luke 10:34 and James 5:14 it was used in connection with healing the sick. Matthew, Mark and Luke reveal that the anointing with oil was also used for preparing the dead for burial.

We call this act a sacrament because it is a formal or holy event that sets forth (to believers) the grace of God in Christ and the blessings of the New Covenant. More to the point, it is the real presence of the Spirit of Christ in this event or occasion that makes it a sacred time or a sacrament.

197. WHY IS OIL USED IN THIS SACRAMENT?

Oil that has been properly prepared is used for anointing because, as such, it is a symbol of joy, prosperity and liberty. Moreover, it speaks of health and symbolizes the Holy Spirit of God.

(Ps. 23:5; Joel 1:10; Micah 6:15)

1 Then Samuel took a vial of oil, and poured it upon his head, and kissed him, and said, Is it not because the Lord hath anointed thee to be captain over his inheritance?

5 After that thou shalt come to the hill of God, where is the garrison of the Philistines: and it shall come to pass, when thou art come thither to the city, that thou shalt meet a company of prophets coming down from the high place with a psaltery, and a tabret, and a pipe, and a harp, before them; and they shall prophesy:

6 And the spirit of the Lord will come upon thee, and thou shalt prophesy with them, and shalt be turned into another man.

I Samuel 10:1, 5-6

Then Samuel took the horn of oil, and anointed him in the midst of his brethren: and the spirit of the Lord came upon David from that day forward So Samuel rose up, and went to Ramah.

I Samuel 16:13

198. WHAT SPECIAL PREPARATION IS REQUIRED BEFORE OIL CAN BE USED IN THE SACRAMENT?

Before the olive oil can be used in the Sacrament it must be blessed or consecrated.

22 Moreover the Lord spake to Moses, saying:

23 "Also take for yourself quality spices — five hundred shekels of liquid myrrh, half as much sweet cinnamon (two hundred and fifty shekels) two hundred and fifty shekels of sweet-smelling cane ,

24 Five hundred shekels of cassia, according to the shekel of the sanctuary, and a hin of olive oil.

25 And you shall make from these a holy anointing oil, an ointment compounded according to the art of the perfumer. It shall be a holy anointing oil.

Exodus 30:22-25 NKJV

The following prayer may be used to bless the oil:

Prayer to Bless the Oil

"Holy Father in heaven, Giver of health and Salvation, Lord, send your Holy Spirit to sanctify this oil, so that, as your holy Apostles anointed the sick and healed them, so may those who, in faith and repentance, receive this holy anointing be made perfectly whole. May it also be that whatever is set apart unto God for His blessing and grace (by the Sacrament of Anointing with oil) that it may indeed be blessed in the precious name of our Lord and Savior, Jesus Christ. Amen."

199. WHO THEN CAN ADMINISTER THIS SACRAMENT, ACCORDING TO THE SCRIPTURES?

A. The Elders of the Church may administer the anointing with oil.

Is anyone among you sick? Let him call for the elders of the church, and let them pray over him, anointing him with oil in the name of the Lord.

James 5:14 NKJV

B. Any true disciple of Jesus Christ may preach the Word, exercise power over unclean spirits, and anoint the sick with oil.

12 So they went out and preached that people should repent.

> *13 and they cast out many demons, and anointed with oil many who were sick, and healed them.*
>
> Mark 6:12-13 NKJV

See also Mark 16:14-20.

Note!

It is not uncommon to see Full Gospel Christians (laymen and clergymen) carrying a small bottle of blessed oil for the purpose of ministry.

200. EXPLAIN THE PURPOSE OF ANOINTING THE SICK WITH OIL. WHY IS THIS DONE?

Physical health is an important part of wholeness and well-being; consequently the Church provides ministry (through this sacrament) for those believers who are battling sickness, disease, old age and even death.

The Apostle James teaches that the sick or afflicted person should call for the Elders of the Church. Sometimes this is impossible. Because of the severity of the condition it may be necessary that someone else call for the Elders.

The Elders are to rub oil upon the sick person and then pray the prayer of faith, calling on the Name of the Lord. The promise of God is that "the prayer of faith shall save (deliver, heal, restore, make whole, liberate) the sick and if he or she has committed any sins, they shall be forgiven."

> *14 Is any among you sick? He should call in the church elders (the spiritual guides). And they should pray over him, anointing him with oil in the Lord's name.*

15 And the prayer [that is] of faith will save him who is sick, and the Lord will restore him; and if he has committed sins, he will be forgiven.

James 5: 14-15 AMP

201. WHY DO SOME CHURCHES ANOINT WITH OIL THOSE WHO ARE CRITICALLY ILL AND AT THE POINT OF DEATH?

Many Christian Churches anoint the seriously ill, just before death, as a kind of "last rite". The focus is upon bringing forgiveness and healing to the inner man and all of this is as a preparation for death and meeting the Lord in the after life.

The minister prays over the one to be anointed saying, "Through this holy anointing, O Lord, in your great mercy and everlasting love, please help my dear brother/sister with the grace of your Holy Spirit, in the Name of Jesus Christ our Lord. Amen."

The minister may further say, "As you are outwardly anointed with this holy oil, so may our heavenly Father grant you the inward anointing of the Holy Spirit. Of His great mercy may He forgive you your sins, release you from suffering, and restore you to wholeness and strength. May He deliver you from all evil, preserve you in all goodness, and bring you to everlasting life; through Jesus Christ our Lord. Amen."

202. WHAT ABOUT THE ANOINTING OF PEOPLE OTHER THAN THOSE WHO ARE SICK OR DYING? WHY ANOINT CARS, HOMES AND OTHER MATERIAL OBJECTS?

Actually, by the practice of anointing with oil, we may consecrate people; places and things unto God.

(Gen. 28:18; Ex 30:26 ff.; I Samuel 9:16; Ex. 28:41)

The Scriptures list the following items as material things that were anointed and thus set apart unto God:

A. Tent/Tabernacle	Lev. 8:10
B. Altar	Ex. 29:36
C. Furniture/utensils	Lev. 8:10-11
D. Laver	Ex. 40:9-16
E. Cakes	Lev. 7:12

In addition to these items, the following persons were anointed:

F. High Priest	Ex. 29:7
G. Prophets	I Kg. 19:16
H. Kings	II Sam. 2:4
I. The dead	Mk. 14:8; 16:1
J. Special guests	Lk. 7:46
K. Ministers	II Cor. 1:21

203. AS NEW COVENANT BELIEVERS, HOW ARE WE TO DEAL WITH THIS SACRAMENT?

First of all, in the Old Testament, only special persons were anointed for service. In the New Testament, all believers are anointed by the Holy One for ministry in the Church.

But you have an anointing from the Holy One, and you know all things.

I John 2:20 NKJV

Secondly, insofar as the anointing with oil is a "means of grace", then New Covenant believers should not hesitate to receive the favor and enabling of God (coming to them by way of this sacrament) by faith.

Conclusion

Thus we may conclude this lesson by remembering that the Law of Contact and Transmission is alive and well. Moreover, the power of our faith declaration and actions produce astounding results. What this means, as far as the Sacrament of Anointing with Oil is concerned, is that whatever you (as a true child of God) anoint, and set apart unto God for His service will surely be blessed and sanctified. You actually have that kind of favor with the King of the Universe.

Lesson Twenty-Six

Matthew 25:19-23 NIV

19 "After a long time the master of those servants returned and settled accounts with them. 20 The man who had received the five talents brought the other five. 'Master,' he said, 'you entrusted me with five talents. See, I have gained five more.'

21 "His master replied, 'Well done, good and faithful servant! You have been faithful with a few things; I will put you in charge of many things. Come and share your master's happiness!'

22 "The man with the two talents also came. 'Master,' he said, 'you entrusted me with two talents; see, I have gained two more.'

23 "His master replied, 'Well done, good and faithful servant! You have been faithful with a few things; I will put you in charge of many things. Come and share your master's happiness!'

CHRISTIAN STEWARDSHIP

The subject of stewardship, as far as the Christian is concerned, has to do with the wise administration of God's creation and grace. This being the case, it then becomes immediately clear that financial matters, though certainly a part of the subject, are none-the-less far from being the only issue at stake. Under this heading of stewardship, the vital questions of Godly character, moral, and spiritual responsibility, as well as accountability, must be dealt with. Only by so approaching the subject at hand is it really possible to understand what "Thus saith the Lord" in this respect.

204. SPECIFICALLY, WHAT IS STEWARDSHIP ALL ABOUT?

In a nutshell, stewardship has to do with the exercise of delegated authority and oversight of property that belongs to someone other than ourselves. Such responsibility is bordered by accountability. We must answer to the owner, or Lord, as to how we managed "His" property. Note the following examples of stewardship arrangements given in the Bible:

A. Potiphar and Joseph [Gen. 39:4]

B. Pharaoh and Joseph [Gen. 41:39-45]

C. I Corinthians 4:1-2

205. WHO IS THE REAL OWNER OF ALL THINGS?

The Scriptures are clear that God is the owner of all things.

A. God owns the earth by creation [cp. Gen. 1:1; Jn. 1:1-3; Ps. 24:1].

B. God owns the earth by redemption.

(1) The creation was made subject to divine judgment as a result of Adam's disobedience [cp. Gen. 3:17-19; Rom. 8:20-22].

(2) Through the redemptive work of Christ, ownership has reverted back to the Father [cp. Rom. 8:16-17; Col. 2:13-15]

206. WHAT DOES OUR PERSONAL CHARACTER HAVE TO DO WITH STEWARDSHIP?

Because that which the Father entrusts to us is of great value, then it stands to reason that He will not allow just anybody to watch over "His" treasure.

A. A good steward must be loyal, well disciplined, obedient, and productive. [cp. Mt. 21:33-41; II Kg. 5]

B. A good steward must always be mindful of the owner's rights. [cp. Ps. 100:3; Jn. 17]

C. Observe! The wisdom, ability, and faithfulness of the steward will have a bearing on just how much responsibility or oversight he'll receive. [Mt. 25:14-30]

207. HOW ARE WE TO UNDERSTAND OUR RESPONSIBILITY IN FINANCES?

God expects us to pay our tithes (10 percent of our income) and give an offering. This is His basic financial plan for His people in all dispensations.

A. The Patriarchs tithed. [cp. Gen. 14:18-20; 28:22]

B. Tithing was included in the Law. [cp. Lev. 27:30, 32; Num. 1:24-26]

C. All the Israelites tithed and gave an offering. [cp. Dt. 12:6, 17; II Chron. 31:5-6, 12; Prov. 3:9-10; Mal. 3:8-12]

D. Jesus endorsed tithing. [Mt. 23:23]

According to the Scriptures, the tithes belong to the Lord and are used primarily in the area of the ministry. [cp. Num. 18:20-28; I Cor. 9:9-14; I Tim. 5:17-18] Moreover, it is necessary to see that the local Christian church is "the storehouse" where new covenant saints pay their tithes. Tithes must not be sent or given to so called evangelistic associations, television ministries, or "Christian causes."

208. WHAT ABOUT OFFERINGS?

A According to Exodus 25:1-9 and Exodus 36:5-6, Moses received offerings for the building of the Tabernacle.

B. In I Chronicles 29:1-14, David rebuilt the temple with offerings.

C. In Matthew 6, Proverbs 19:17, Mark 10:29-30 and Luke 6:38, we learn that offerings may be earmarked for the poor and needy, the Gospel ministry, and for the Praise to God. Based on the sowing and reaping principle, all such giving will yield tremendous dividends.

209. SHOULD A CHRISTIAN (WHO IS COMMITTED TO A LIFE OF TOTAL FAITH IN GOD) DO ANY FINANCIAL PLANNING?

Yes! God makes plans. In other words, God is an orderly provider, and He expects to see orderliness in his people. The Christian home (or family) should be characterized by financial orderliness and excellence; however, neither of these qualities will show up accidentally or automatically. Good planning is necessary.

210. WHAT STEPS TO FINANCIAL PLANNING SHOULD CHRISTIANS BE TAKING?

1. **Write down your plan or budget.**

This will provide you with a visible objective standard to work toward.

Suggested Budget Percentage Guidelines

Gross Income per month: $_____

Minus:

Tithe (10% of Gross)
Tax (12% of Gross)
equals:

Net Spendable Income: $_____

Expenses:

   Housing (27 % of Net) $_____
   Food (10% of Net) $_____
   Auto (15% of Net) $_____

Insurance (10% of Net) $_____
Debts (5 % of Net) $_____
Entertainment &
 recreation (7 % of Net) $_____
Clothing (5 % of Net) $_____
Savings (10% of Net) $_____
Medical/Dental (5 % of Net) $_____
Miscellaneous (6% of Net) $_____
Total: (Cannot Exceed
 Net Spendable Income) $_____

2. Pay your tithes first.

(See Financial Priority Chart) Prov. 3:9-10: II Cor. 9:11

3. Cut down on credit buying. (Prov. 22:7)

4. Live within your budget.

Overspending causes more family problems than insufficient income. Before deciding to take on another job or before sending your wife into the work force, correct your bad spending habits. Remember to put your faith to work in the area of your finances. Make it your policy to pray about *every* expenditure.

> For which of you, intending to build a tower, sitteth not down first, and counteth the cost, whether he have sufficient to finish it?
>
> Luke 14:28 KJV

5. Don't allow other people to establish your financial plans and goals and avoid "get-rich-quick" schemes! Use wisdom in your decision making. In the eighth Proverb the writer has Wisdom speak to us saying,

> 17 I love those who love me and those who seek me find me.
>
> 18 With me are riches and honor, enduring wealth and prosperity.
>
> 19 My fruit is better than fine gold; what I yield surpasses choice silver.
>
> 20 I walk in the way of righteousness, along the paths of justice,
>
> 21 bestowing wealth upon those who love me and making their treasuries full.
>
> Proverbs 8:17-21 NIV

> 13 Blessed is the man who finds wisdom, the man who gains understanding,
>
> 14 for she is more profitable than silver and yields better returns than gold.
>
> Proverbs 3:13-14 NIV

6. Get good Christian counsel.

Sometimes the advice we need resides within our family members. Your spouse should be consulted on all major purchases. If you are not married, you might consider talking things over with your Christian parents, God parents or guardian.

> Where no counsel is, the people fall: but in the multitude of counsellors there is safety.
>
> Proverbs 11:14

Hear counsel, and receive instruction, that thou mayest be wise in thy latter end.

Proverbs 19:20

Harken unto thy father that begat thee, and despise not thy mother when she is old.

Proverbs 23:22

24 Therefore as the church is subject unto Christ, so let the wives be to their own husbands in every thing.

31 For this cause shall a man leave his father and mother, and shall be joined unto his wife, and they two shall be one flesh.

Ephesians 5:24, 31

7. Establish a standard of living for your family.

The cultivation of the inner self is of greater value, in the eyes of God, than the adornment of the outward man. God recognizes that we have need of things and He moreover promises to meet that need.

31 Therefore take no thought, saying, What shall we eat? or, What shall we drink? or, Wherewithal shall we be clothed?

32 (For after all these things do the Gentiles seek:) for your heavenly Father knoweth that ye have need of all these things.

33 But seek ye first the kingdom of God, and his righteousness; and all these things shall be added unto you.

Matthew 6:31-33

However, you must be able to distinguish between needs, wants/desires and lavishness. Every basic purchase in the home should be evaluated in light of these categories and either allowed or disallowed according to your family plan or budget.

As you go about setting your family standard of living and financial goals, make sure your heart attitude is right. Make sure you are seeking first the Kingdom of God and His righteousness and not the things of the world to be used only for personal gain. (I Tim. 6:6-8; I Jn: 2:15-17; Lk 3:11)

8. Save some money.

How much does it take for your family to function for one month? You should have at least this amount of money saved. Enough for three to six months would be even better. This savings would only be used if the breadwinner becomes incapacitated. Once this fund is in place, you can begin to save for other designated goals — retirement, new home, car down payment, family vacation, etc., etc., etc.

In the house of the wise are stores of choice food and oil, but a foolish man devours all he has.

Proverbs 21:20 NIV

9. Leave an inheritance.

Our Covenant obligation to our family extends beyond death. The Apostle Paul taught that one who didn't take care of his family was worse than an unsaved heathen.

A good man leaves an inheritance to his children's children. But the wealth of the sinner is stored up for the righteous.

Proverbs 13:22 NKJV

211. DOES THE BIBLE SAY ANYTHING ABOUT SHARING OUR GIFTS AND CONTRIBUTIONS WITH OTHERS IN THE COVENANT COMMUNITY?

Yes! God's plan for sharing starts with the tithe and then moves on to helping those around us who have obvious needs. Beyond this, we are taught to give out of our abundance or surplus. Finally, we are urged to give sacrificially, that is we are taught to (at times) give up our personal wants and needs in order to help others.

Sacrificial giving requires the "God kind of love" to be in operation. Christians who have a surplus, need to recognize that surplus as God's blessing to them, and they should seek His will regarding how it should be used.

(Mt. 25:33-40; Jas. 2:15; II Cor. 8:12-15; Lk. 21:1-4; Heb. 13:16; II Cor. 8:7- 9)

212. WHO ARE SOME OF THE PEOPLE WHO <u>DO NOT</u> DESERVE OUR HELP? WHAT DOES THE WORD SAY?

Some people are not to be helped! To do so would interfere with God's dealings in their lives. To do so will also tend to bless what God is really judging.

10 For even when we were with you, we commanded you, that if any would not work, neither should he eat.

11 For we hear that there are some which walk among you disorderly, working not at all, but are busy bodies.

12 Now them that are such we command and exhort by our Lord Jesus Christ, that with quietness they work, and eat their own bread.

II Thessalonians 3:10-12

213. WHO DOES DESERVE HELP?

1. Your Family

The Scriptures teach that a family is more than a husband, wife and children, It is also other relatives such as mother, father, aunts, uncles, etc. All of those are deserving of our help, provided that they cannot meet their own needs.

(I Tim.5:8, 16; Mt. 15: 5-6)

Note!

The government is not responsible for providing for family members who cannot provide for themselves.

2. The Body of Christ
(Jas. 2:15-16)

17 But whoso hath this world's good and seeth his brother have need, and shutteth up his bowels of compassion from him, how dwelleth the love of God in him?

18 My Little Children, let us not love in word, neither in tongue; but in deed and in truth.

I John 3:17-18

3. Shepherds/Elders
(III Jn. 5-6)

For it is written in the law of Moses, Thou shalt not muzzle the mouth of the ox that treadeth out the corn. Doth God take care for oxen?

Or saith he it altogether for our sakes ? For our sakes, no doubt, this is written: that he that ploweth should plow in hope; and that he that thresheth in hope should be partaker of his hope.

If we have sown unto you spiritual things, is it a great thing if we shall reap your carnal things?

I Corinthians 9:9-11

4. The Unsaved

We are to witness not only by our words but by our actions as well. (Mt. 10:42)

Give to him that asketh thee, and from him that would borrow of thee turn not thou away.

Matthew 5:42

Conclusion

God has made his Covenant People stewards over all of His creation. We are therefore obligated to take care of His "property" in a manner that is in accordance with the desires of His heart. In other words we are to follow God's guidelines for the proper care and nurture of everything that belongs to Him.

We each belong to the Father individually. He has created us and redeemed us by the blood of the Lamb. Every second we live, every breath we take belongs to God. We have been created for His good pleasure and to bring Him glory. One of the things that gives God pleasure is the prosperity of His servants. Throughout the Scriptures, God makes it very plain that He not only wants His people to prosper but that He will take an active part in seeing to it that we do just that! As a servant of the Most High God, we do not have the right to be poor!

It is the will of the Father that, as He blesses us, we are to become a channel of blessing to others. In His Word, it is laid out quite clearly how we are to handle the wealth God has in store for us. First, we are to pay the tithe (for which we get a blessing). We are to render unto the government those funds that are due it. We are to take good care of our families and make few debts but handle those few with integrity. Then when we get into the realm of surplus, (Hallelujah!) we get to be used by God to help finance the maintenance and furtherance of the Kingdom; we get to tangibly show love to our brothers and sisters in need; underwrite ministry needs in the church; finance missionary and evangelistic outreach; utterly destroy lack in the household of faith.

Endnotes

[1] Minutes of the 44th session of the General council of the Assemblies of God with revised constitution and bylaws (Springfield, MO.: The General council of the Assemblies of God, 1991), p. 129.

[2] Ibid.

www.ingramcontent.com/pod-product-compliance
Lightning Source LLC
Chambersburg PA
CBHW071144160426
43196CB00011B/2006